Sexual Arrangements

ALSO BY M. P. M. RICHARDS

The Integration of a Child into a Social World (editor), 1974

Infancy: The World of the Newborn, 1980

Children of Social Worlds (edited with Paul Light), 1986

Divorce Matters (with Jacqueline Burgoyne
and Roger Ormrod), 1987

The Politics of Maternity Care (edited with Jo Garcia
and Robert Kilpatrick)

Sexual Arrangements

Marriage and the Temptation of Infidelity

Janet Reibstein, Ph.D.
Martin Richards, Ph.D.

CHARLES SCRIBNER'S SONS NEW YORK
MAXWELL MACMILLAN CANADA TORONTO
MAXWELL MACMILLAN INTERNATIONAL
NEW YORK OXFORD SINGAPORE SYDNEY

Charles Scribner's Sons
Macmillan Publishing Company
866 Third Avenue
New York, NY 10022

Maxwell Macmillan Canada, Inc.
1200 Eglinton Avenue East
Suite 200
Don Mills, Ontario M3C 3N1

Macmillan Publishing Company is part of the Maxwell Communication Group of Companies.

Library of Congress Cataloging-in-Publication Data
Reibstein, Janet Alese.
Sexual arrangements : marriage and the temptation of infidelity /
    Janet Reibstein and Martin Richards.
        p. cm.
    Includes bibliographical references and index.
    ISBN 0-684-19540-2
    1. Adultery. 2. Marriage.   I. Richards, Martin Paul Meredith.
    II. Title.
    HQ806.R45 1993
    306.73'6—dc20   93-12151   CIP

Macmillan books are available at special discounts for bulk purchases for sales promotions, premiums, fund-raising, or educational use. For details, contact:

Special Sales Director
Macmillan Publishing Company
866 Third Avenue
New York, NY 10022

10 9 8 7 6 5 4 3 2 1

Printed in the United States of America

For my family
J. R.

Contents

Acknowledgments

This book is the product of a collaboration across disciplines and professional roles. While the first author draws on her experience as a therapist and a psychologist who has researched both psychotherapy and relationships, the second uses his background as a social scientist, particularly as a researcher on divorce, sexual development, and parents and children. We believe that our approaches are complimentary and that the different knowledge, assumptions, and experience we have each contributed have created a better argument than the simple sum of its two parts. Our writing was preceded—and followed—by long hours of discussion. One of us has taken primary responsibility for each chapter (J.R. 1, 2, 5, 6, and 7, M.R. 3, 4, 8, and 9) but the final version is the result of much rewriting by both of us.

We would both like to thank the many individuals and couples who have generously shared their accounts of their marriages and other relationships with us. They have provided an invaluable resource for our thinking and writing. We are also greatly indebted to all those colleagues, friends, and students with whom we have discussed, argued, and rehearsed our ideas. They have stimulated our thinking, extended our knowledge, and helped us to clarify our arguments. Sally Roberts and Jill Brown have typed all too many versions of the manuscript and have moved between three word processing systems with great skill. Similarly we would like to thank our agent, Gail Hochman, and our editor, Bill Goldstein, for their energy and insights, and who handled the difficulties of transatlantic communication with grace and good humor.

The first author's family, including her husband, Stephen Monsell, whose support and often wry insights were invaluable, and two young sons, Adam and Daniel Monsell, who adapted cheerfully to the sometimes unfair demands of that third child, the book, merit profound and lasting admiration and gratitude.

The second author would like to thank Jane Elliott, who has been his collaborator in his recent divorce research. Among other assistance, she was responsible for clarifying the concept of her and his divorces. He has always found the process of writing, and the reading and thought that precedes it, a lonely business and owes a special debt to the familiar voices of Billie Jo, Crystal, Emmylou, Holly, K.T., Nanci, Tanya, Wynonna and Naomi.

We would like to thank the following publishers, agents and authors for permission to quote from their work: Harcourt Brace Jovanovich, Philip Larkin, "Annus Mirabilis"; The Dial Press, The Wendy Weil Agency, Inc., Jane Lazarre, *On Loving Men*; Jonathon Cape, Ann Oakley, *Taking It Like a Woman*.

The excerpt from "Remember You're Mine" by Mann and Lowe is reproduced by kind permission of Warner Chappell Music, Inc.

We offer our apologies to any copyright owners who, despite our best efforts, we have been unable to locate.

Sexual Arrangements

1

Introduction

Do not adultery commit;
Advantage rarely comes of it.

Arthur Hugh Clough (1819–1861), *The Latest Decalogue*

Accursed from birth they be
Who seek to find monogamy,
Pursuing it from bed to bed—
I think they would be better dead.

Dorothy Parker, *Not So Deep as a Well* (1937)

FOR MANY MONTHS SAM WAS IN LOVE. FLASHES OF ELLEN, HER smile, her body, shivers of her scent, and fragments of their days and nights together floated in and out of his day, inflating him with longing, with fondness, and with desire.

Sam is forty-two. He is a successful investment banker. He surveys the world's money markets from a large mahogany desk on the top floor of an impressive building in a major financial center. You might have passed him on his daily train commute, wearing his stylish dark blue suit and pure silk tie, or have observed him trading jokes with colleagues or chairing meetings with solemn aplomb, and never guessed at the images of Ellen jostling for attention with banking figures in his brain. You would not have guessed because Ellen, powerful as she was for him, was a secret. For Sam is married—to somebody else. Like so many others who have affairs, Sam's with Ellen was secret. Now, years later, after Sam and Ellen have both put each other and their affair far away, their affair has remained secret. Sam is still married. He hopes his affair will *never* come to light.

Christina was also in love and sleeping with someone who was not her husband. She, too, watched over her secret, carrying it like a tune as she went through her day teaching dance classes, picking up the children, doing the shopping, cooking the meals. But one day the carefully constructed walls around her romantic idyll split asunder: somebody knew and was threatening to tell. So Christina confessed to her husband, and overnight a passionate love affair turned into a tragic and painful mess. Her husband's friendship with her former lover is forever destroyed; her marriage survives but remains shaken to the core.

Ursula and David are also having affairs. They, too, are married, and they are married to each other. Each knows about the other's affair, and each says that the other's affair enriches their life together. Ursula, too, lives as if with an extra sense, an ever-present sexuality now that she is sleeping with Sean. The image of herself as an "adulteress" excites her, and for the first time since the beginning of their marriage she and David have had exciting, inventive sex. Meanwhile, David is also feeling "tingly," as he describes it, from his latest "crush" (again, his word). He is also in love, and the feeling that he is alive with love suffuses the rest of his world with it. As he sees it, in large part because of their affairs, he and Ursula are brimming with sexuality together, and this despite a small town house teeming with three small and demanding children, two active careers, and a history of deep affection but unexciting sex.

And then there is Annie, who slept with a man other than her husband while on a self-awareness vacation. She was not in love. Indeed, she felt something like contempt for the man with whom she had slept. Or investment banker Sam again, who once slept with a secretary provided to him on a business trip, and though he thought she was attractive, he had no interest in repeating the experience.

We could go on. Examples are rife in life and in literature, in movies, and on television. Indeed, wherever there is a story of a marriage there could be a story of an affair. David, Ursula, Sam, Annie, Christina—they are all having or have had affairs. Yet, despite some similarities, their affairs are different, carried on for different reasons, inspiring different feelings, and leaving very different marks on them.

If any of these people were our friends, colleagues, or neighbors we would probably find ourselves shocked to discover their affairs. For affairs, in themselves, shock. They represent what we are not supposed to do. While preparing this book, when we told colleagues and acquaintances the subject matter under study, as often as not we encountered raised eyebrows, low chuckles, and embarrassed silences. People tend to miss a beat before asking further questions. Affairs bring other people up short. Yet most people either know someone close to them who has had an affair, have had one themselves, endured their spouse having one, or, before marriage, were the third party in one. If they fail to fall into one of these four categories, normally they do fall into a fifth: they have thought about having an affair, or have *almost* had an affair themselves.

Still, despite their prevalence, despite the tug of fascination with the idea of affairs, people do not understand them. They do not know why people have them—although they can tell you why they should not—or what they get from having them, or even what an affair is. Are David's and Ursula's affairs the same as Christina's? Should the two we've described for Sam be lumped together and share the label "affair"?

What all these people do have in common is the fact that they are married. Almost all have been happily married at some time, though probably none thought this at the time of the affair. They once shared something else: a belief in the all-embracing, transforming power of marriage. Apart from Ursula and David, they continue to share a belief in monogamy. Each entered marriage with the firm belief that marriage should be forever. Whether written by them or in words of traditional services, each spoke vows shot through with a deep conviction: marriage provides a salve for wounds brought on by living, is a place in which lust is endlessly sated, and friendship and warmth always abound.

This is how most of us enter marriage. Yet approximately half of us will have an extramarital affair. Most of us will seriously contemplate one. Are so many of us morally corrupt? Are we, in such vast numbers, terminally foolish? Are those who unravel the fabric of the monogamy that is supposed to support their marriage all horribly misguided? Or are many of those who have affairs perhaps fumbling to come to some sort of arrangement? Are they trying to strike some kind of a deal—however shaky and mistaken in some cases—with the complex intertwining of lives in the marriages in which they find themselves? We suggest that the fault lies in the beliefs we keep trying to sustain about marriage, even in the face of conflicting experience. Perhaps it is the unchanging and unrealistic expectations of our marriages that propel more than half of married couples into mostly secret affairs.

Up to now affairs have been attributed mainly to moral corruption or pathology. We disagree. We think it is inadequate to explain the multitude of affairs in our society, increasingly documented in growing numbers of studies, by summoning up visions of millions of separate, personal pathologies: inadequate people unable to commit themselves to a single, demanding relationship because of one deficiency or other. Affairs occur so often that they begin to take on something like a "normal" quality, if we define normal at least in terms of statistical frequency. It seems implausible to argue that we are producing in numbers approaching "normal" so many pathologically deficient people. So we look elsewhere—to the institution against which these people seem to be reacting—marriage. Nobody wants to be unfaithful. But nobody wants to be unhappy in marriage, either.

Most of the time affairs represent a balancing act. They are the deals struck between maintaining a marriage, albeit one that has only part of what one expected it to have, on the one hand, and satisfying individual needs believed to be (sometimes wrongly so) incompatible with the marriage, on the other. Affairs lead to a range of feelings and outcomes, as we shall see. But those feelings invariably include a sense of failure or regret about not having the perfect marriage—that romantic, cocooning and still lust-filled friendship—after all.

The failure, as we see it, is chiefly the failure of the ideal. We

have no model flowing from that ideal that accounts for the difficult days, months, and years of a lived-in marriage. The frictions of
the early days—who washes the dishes and when and how well—
can lead to dejection and disenchantment; the sleepless nights of
the early childbearing years can lead to months of perfunctory,
infrequent, and often less than joyous lovemaking; the resentments
of bearing up under the same never-resolved conflicts over the years
can lead to dejection and alienation from the pleasure of a partner's
company by middle age. Our ideal leaves us feeling cheated or like
failures. Of course we can "settle"; we can settle for less than we
bargained for, less than the advertised best. But isn't that a failure, a
cheat? We feel vulnerable because our model of what to strive for in
marriage is a weak and vulnerable one.

There is another factor. We are a very eroticized society, as seen
not only in films, novels, advertisements, and television but also in
the increasing number of people who are having sex with each
other. Men and women do not arrive at their marriages as blank
slates. They have histories, and today these are usually sexual ones.
Relationships between men and women before marriage, more
often than in past generations, end up in bed. Our grandmothers
probably did not sleep with our grandfathers before their wedding
night and almost certainly did not sleep with anyone else. Our
grandfathers might have had some perfunctory sexual experiences,
but even they were much more likely to be virgins at their weddings. Now most women and men have had sex before marriage. It
has also been a rising trend for those marrying to have had more
than one lover before marriage, and in some cases many (although
we await more current statistics on this given the effect of AIDS).

The age at which sexual intercourse first occurs is also decreas-
ing. By the end of the eighties a majority of girls were leaving high
school no longer virgins. Heterosexual relationships are now charged
with innuendo and potential. Yet suddenly, when we marry,
although we continue to have social relationships outside of marriage, we are not allowed to think of others "that way." "That" is
permitted only for our spouses. The problem is that of course we do
think of others in that way. A sexually charged relationship between
two people not married to each other, combined with disillusionment with marriage—disillusionment that any married person nor-

mally experiences at points in any marriage—can ignite into an affair.

Our marital ideal has not always been as it is today, nor is it the one exalted in non-Western cultures. Just a century ago marriage represented a coming together of families in property or possessions, an unequal partnership of a man and woman in which the husband was the boss. It meant the joining of two people perhaps in love but not necessarily in intimate friendship and certainly not with expectations of equal sexual bliss. Over the past one hundred years a new ideal has gradually evolved, one that encompasses most significantly the changes in women's roles, sexual experiences, educational pursuits, and working lives. A companionate model that idealizes intimacy, support, and friendship and that demands a partnership of mutually satisfying sex has grown up.

Just a century ago people did not live as long as they do now. Marriages then did not potentially span half a century. As we have said, the ideal marriage is now that of the perfectly enriching partnership, endlessly satisfying. Over a short period this would be difficult enough. Over the longer lifetime of a marriage—often decades longer than our great-great-grandparents'—this is a very tall order, a greater demand on modern marriage.

This ideal that has evolved and that is not supposed to vary over the lifetime of very long marriages does not give even a passing nod to the wear and tear in any partnership, let alone one joined at so many seams as marriage. It does not acknowledge the tensions that exist when the interests of the individual are at odds with those of the couple. It does not acknowledge change or tension; it is only about togetherness, intimacy at the expense of autonomy. People push against these restraints in different ways. We suggest that affairs, which must remain secret to preserve the marriage, represent one of those ways.

Another way, much touted during the late sixties and early seventies, is the "open marriage," in which individual growth is vaunted over that of the partnership. Research on marriages of this sort suggests that this was and still is very much a minority response, with marriages often ending or changing back again to the more conventional model. Monogamy remains very much a fixed goal, it seems, and the marital ideal of partnership rather than attention to individual needs is very much entrenched. So we are back to the solution this book addresses: affairs, most of which remain secret, during marriage.

We believe that secrecy is at the heart of most affairs. It is necessary since the ideal espouses the sharing of everything—particularly anything important—and monogamy. Not giving up the ideal, we know we are acting against it, and so, if we have affairs, we are guilty. We are betraying. We must keep them secret. But in that secrecy lies much of the reason that affairs are so powerful. Secrecy protects the forbidden, which especially in contrast to the familiar is an aphrodisiac. Secrecy gives power: "I have something you do not know about." Secrecy guards autonomy, the part of the self that is inviolably (as long as it remains secret) separate from one's spouse. And secrecy keeps the marriage afloat, for discovery clearly might sink it.

It is also this secrecy, we believe, that erodes marriages as much as the affair itself. Undiscovered affairs, which may well be the bulk of them, are not those normally destructive of marriages. Of course they can destroy as much as they can enhance or even not measurably affect marriages, as chapter 7 shows. But secrecy and sex outside marriage potentially erode the intimacy of marriage. Moreover, the effects of discovering a secret affair erode the base of marital trust. However, that secrecy can also save a marriage. As long as secrecy remains, marital pain and turmoil may be avoided. Through this conundrum, which secrecy in affairs highlights, we can see that the ideals of intimacy and monogamy, cornerstones of modern marriage, while noble and enhancing for many, ironically contain the very germ that others discover is the seed of its own destruction.

We believe there is a psychological basis for the development of both our monogamous, intimate marital ideal as well as for the different needs men and women are seeking to address through their affairs. Most psychological theorists agree that the crucible for our emotional development is the mother-infant relationship. All else is secondary. The infant needs his or her mother to satisfy his or her changing developmental needs with consistency. The mother or mother-figure—and in our society this is invariably a woman—is the baby's world. From this world the baby branches out, gradually expanding it and becoming separate from the mother. This is how

the "self" develops—first merged in a secure, undifferentiated relationship with the mother and then gradually moving away from her.
That one-to-one, intense, all-satisfying, and dependable original
relationship sets the pattern out of which all later love will be cut.
The intense attachment of love—and our formal structure for it,
marriage—recalls the yearning to be loved and to love in that first
and exclusive dependent and dependable way. Whether the mother
did indeed satisfy her infant is immaterial. The expectations
remain. If she did satisfy, one knows that such exclusive and fulfilling love exists; if she did not, one still craves it.

Historians of the family have shown that since Victorian times
our child-rearing practices and expectations have radically changed,
along with marriage, making such expectations of mother-child
exclusivity inevitable. We have come to expect the child's mother
to be exclusively responsible. Legions of single-parent families are
centered around the mother, often without other family on whom
to depend for help or relief and sometimes with absolutely no contact with fathers. Less than a century ago in lower-class families
members of the extended family shared the work of child care, while
in upper-class ones servants helped mothers, who shared with
fathers a more distant if emotionally distinctive and important role.
More than ever in the latter half of this century we have emphasized the centrality of the maternal role, gradually pushing paternal
responsibility to the periphery of a child's emotional development.
The romantic ideal of the intense, one-to-one monogamous fulfillment of marriage has its psychological roots in the mother-focused,
one-to-one mother-child way we are raised in families in Western
culture today.

A striking thing about affairs we have found is that more women
than ever are having them. On one level this is not surprising, given
the change in women's roles and widening sexual experience. But
on another it is. Women are supposed to need love with sex. Are all
these women in these affairs falling in love time after time?

The answer is not that simple, as we state in chapter 5. Women
may not be in love with all their affair partners, and they may well
be having affairs that are primarily about sex, but they remain less
able than men to separate sex from some form of emotional
involvement, some type of caretaking. This difference between the

sexes is also rooted in our current child-rearing models. It, too, has deep psychological roots. These male-female differences in affairs are also rooted in this currently typical child-rearing model. The mother, the first love, shares the gender of her daughter but not her son. The daughter's struggle to develop a self separated from the mother is greater. Mothers and daughters tend to stay more merged, identified as they are with each other, than sons and mothers since gender is a primary definer both of how we view the world and of how we are viewed by others. It is a basic ingredient of experience shared by mothers and daughters, and it complicates the process of developing a separate self for girls. But it also enhances their ability to feel connected and empathic to others.

The reverse is that a boy can be more separate and sure of his "self"—where he begins and others end. Boys tend to be less identified with others. Separating sex from emotions and cutting themselves off—sometimes appropriately but sometimes not—from others is easier for them than for girls. Men can have more affairs that they describe as "just sexual" than women, while women, although enjoying the sexual part of them perhaps just as much, tend to become "involved" more often. Psychologically, men can turn away from affairs more easily than women, who still think about their lovers while they move on to the next thing claiming their attention. We see this as a gender difference very much rooted in the fact that mothers, in a deep sense, are our first loves and first worlds, given that gender is so basic to experience.

The Origin of the Book

This book began as a response to the dearth of adequate explanations about affairs, a widespread phenomenon that has such different meanings for men and for women. But it also came about because we kept confronting the issues of affairs and infidelity professionally and, of course, personally. We both have many friends, relatives, and friends of friends who are having affairs. One of us is a psychotherapist whose practice has included couples, many of whom challenged preconceived notions about affairs. Sometimes children were not harmed by affairs, and sometimes they never knew. Sometimes spouses never did find out, and marriages hummed happily along. Sometimes people who seemed utterly without sex appeal were having wild and passionate sex with others (some of whom were themselves buttoned up and inhibited). The other of us was doing research on divorcing couples. Most of them did not immediately cite an affair as the cause of the marital breakdown, but after some probing it became apparent that many of these couples had experienced an affair but did not see it as the reason they could no longer live together. Instead they cited other things, such as lack of communication or sexual incompatibility.

It is notoriously difficult to study affairs. People do not want to admit to having them, and therefore it is very hard to calculate with any degree of accuracy the number of people having them. Studies on attitudes show that most people believe in monogamy. But the studies that exist on people's sexual behavior suggest, as we have said, that perhaps more than half of marriages have an affair.

People do not want to admit to affairs because they clearly do not approve of their own behavior. More than that, if they acknowledge their affairs, they might be discovered, and if discovered, their marriages could be wrecked. So most studies have had to make do with the samples of people they could get recruited either through press advertisements or through something called the "snowball" method (interview one person and get him or her to suggest another person to be interviewed) or through clinical samples, such as people in marital therapy. These are not representative samples; they do not accurately reflect the population at large, since they have been self-selected or selected in other biased ways. Any conclusions drawn from them are therefore shaky and will not necessarily hold for the population at large.

The methodology that best fits a study of affairs is to randomly sample a population of married people. In this, which would represent all married people, some will have had affairs. However, this method poses both ethical and practical problems and is unwieldy and expensive. Questions about affairs stir up conflict within marriages. Privacy and confidentiality are necessary, yet those very conditions can provoke suspicions in spouses or arouse guilt in those who have had affairs. Most funding agencies do not want to be seen as funding a study that some could think invades people's privacy or is sensationalistic. Unfortunately, this attitude is a by-product of the titillation and embarrassment that accompanies the subject of affairs. Officialdom's attitude of refusing to acknowledge the potential usefulness of such a study conspires in the secrecy about affairs. It is also a macro-level manifestation of the underground, secret nature of most of them.

However, judging from the admittedly flawed studies that have been done, we can estimate that between 50 percent and 75 percent of men and a slightly smaller proportion of women have had or are having affairs while married.

This book contains stories gleaned from informal interviews over the past ten years with over two hundred people who have been in affairs while married. Our sample has been an "opportunity" one: we have used a combination of techniques—the snowball method, word-of-mouth, clinical material, and interviews with people who were divorcing. While these interviews have been very important in helping flesh out our ideas, this is not a data-based study. We make no empirical claims. We have chosen instead to think first about affairs theoretically, starting from thinking about marriage. In order to protect the confidentiality and anonymity of the people who so generously spoke to us—sometimes in great distress, other times with equanimity, but always with sincerity and generosity and, as much as we can tell, with often difficult honesty—we have had to change names and identifying details in reporting their stories. We have done so in such a way as to preserve the spirit of the details and the stories. This is always a risk, of course. The details have been changed, however, in such a way as to keep the important factors constant—class, generation, marital status, and educational background are kept the same, while professions may be changed to ones of similar status.

Few people have tried to take a dispassionate view of this phenomenon (or set of phenomena) that we are calling affairs, but fewer still have attempted to explain it in psychological detail. We intend to define and to understand what an affair is, but we will also examine the why of affairs and see what it is about marriage (we all say we want to be monogamous) that might predispose people to having affairs. We will focus on secrecy, the cornerstone of so many and probably most affairs. And we will dissect the difference between men's affairs and women's. One of the great unexamined yet explosive areas of affairs is the influence of the gender divide: man's world/woman's world; her marriage/his marriage; his affair/her affair.

We do not want to oversimplify a rich and complex area of human experience, so we will not attempt to give a single "theory" on affairs. Instead we will look at all the issues—the gender divide, the variations on models of marriage evolved in response to our harsh ideal, the predisposing factors, and the question of secrecy—as ways of getting a better understanding both of affairs and of marriage.

Perhaps most important, as we have already suggested, to write a book about affairs means to write a book about marriage. Without marriage there can be no affair.

The stories that opened this chapter are about people whose tales will be elaborated throughout the book. Each exemplifies something typical about affairs and marriage. We will meet them again as well as hear shorter accounts from others about various aspects of affairs.

Sam, as we have seen, is forty-two, an investment banker, married for twelve years to Marlene, a teacher in an elementary school. They met on a vacation when Sam was first starting out on his high-flying financial career. He was attracted to her exotic good looks, and she to his taciturn strength. Both were thinking about marriage, and the time was right. Sam was never passionate about Marlene, although Marlene has always been sure that Sam is who she wants. They have no children. Instead their house, pets, and Sam's career have occupied Marlene's nurturing talents. Marlene is quiet, unobtrusive, and maternal. She is deeply proud of her husband, respectful of his considerable intellect, and pleased with the fact that he can afford to keep them housed, clothed, and fed.

A major life change combined with reaching middle age and a sustained lack of passion and fulfilling sex in his marriage led Sam into a serious, marriage-threatening affair. Marlene never found out, and so their marriage carries on, much the same on the surface and very much the same to Marlene. Sam's affair illustrates many of the factors that can lead people into affairs and that secret affairs, if left undiscovered, do not necessarily threaten a marriage.

Christina is in her late thirties, married for eleven years and a mother of two. She had been a dancer until an injury left her home-bound with small children. Her life became humdrum, and she lost a sense of her own authority and freedom of choice. She became, she felt, much too dependent on her husband, whom she both loved and resented for his great reserves of energy and competence. When she was in too much pain to manage the children, he would take over, even after a hard day of work. Although he rarely cooked, he was never bothered if she could not manage to bend over a hot stove; he made sandwiches cheerfully and then put the children to bed. Meanwhile he was working, meeting people, and playing sports, and she was not. One thing she had that he did not was quite a bit of sexual experience, but without any opportunity to meet anyone, she began to doubt her attractiveness. Then she had an operation that eradicated her chronic pain and allowed her to begin to reenter the dance world. At the same time her children were old enough not to need her all the time. Christina began to commute to the city for dance events. There she met her first lover, who affirmed her autonomy, her attractiveness, her life apart from her husband. The affair also showed how the period of one's life as well as well as imagined or real inadequacies in a marriage can combine, again with opportunity, to set the scene for an affair, for a woman as well as for a man.

Annie had her first affair much earlier in her marriage. It taught her that being a mother was not incompatible with sexiness. Having small babies can certainly dampen sex lives, as many studies of the early years of marriage attest. Annie's experience bore this out. Moreover, her husband was often cold to her, and although Annie is an extraordinarily attractive woman, she was convinced she was not. Her husband resolutely refused to stroke her vanity. When sex became even more infrequent after her first child, Annie thought sex might well be over for her. Her first affair confirmed that it was her relationship with her husband that was conspiring to make her feel sexually inadequate, not her sexuality. For Annie, affairs became a way of filling the gap between her husband and herself. When her first affair ended, it was not long before a second, a third, then a fourth began. Each filled an ever-yawning marital gap, not only a gap about sex but also about support, intimacy, and friendship.

Linda and Peter, whom we have not yet met, are another couple whose story comes up throughout the book. Linda had an affair with Bill, Peter's colleague. It was passionate, sexually fantastic, very close, wildly emotional, and time-consuming. Linda embarked on it consciously to even an old score with Peter, who had had a brief affair just after their first child was born. Peter called it "just sexual," but Linda was deeply hurt; she had not realized that she had changed the rules of their open marriage after they had become parents. Up until then both of them had had brief affairs. This was in part what we call carryover behavior from the time they were living together, unsure about how committed to each other they were. Carryover behavior may be found in the early years of a marriage when a couple is testing the boundaries of their relationship and still acting as if not fully committed. As a step toward commitment they bought a place together, then eventually took the next step and married. But the permission to have affairs hung on through both steps.

Inchoately, Linda had assumed that having children would forbid affairs. When Peter blithely phoned to announce that she should not expect him home one evening, she was in turmoil but felt unjustified in her despair and anger. After all the unaltered explicit contract permitted him to do just that. Her anger lay buried. The couple drifted apart, fed by that and also because the baby became her domain when she left her job while Peter continued working. Her world shrunk to that of her home and child, and Peter's remained outside. Never one to discuss feelings and always self-reliant and quiet, Peter had increasingly less to say to Linda and less time in which to say it. They became further estranged, and their sex life suffered as well. Linda, on the lookout for a casual fling, was unprepared for the deep, wild way in which she fell for Bill, a divorced man who had admired and desired her from afar. Their affair almost broke up Linda's marriage. Deeply wounded by her own parents' divorce when she was a child, divorce was not an option for Linda. The wild and passionate affair had to end. As we shall see in chapter 7, this proved traumatic, but it was also the first step toward the eventual recovery and strengthening of Linda and Peter's marriage.

Ursula and David are different from the other couples: they have an open marriage. In their early thirties with three children, both are professionals. They met at a prestigious university and are from unconventional, high-profile families with connections to the media. Since both come from families in which parents and parents' friends have had affairs, some highly public, they entered marriage with the understanding that affairs might well happen for them. Both were young when they met and married, and both saw their friends going from relationship to relationship. Neither wanted to believe that the love they felt for each other should restrict their development. They were also probably afraid of sexual boredom, since sex between them did not seem as exciting as they imagined it could be. Their solution was an open marriage. David was the first to have sex with someone outside the marriage. It took Ursula a longer time, but it was done with David's active encouragement. The couple has had live-in nannies and Ursula works sporadically, so it was not until their second child was out of infancy that Ursula found the time to have a weekend away with the man she had picked to be her first lover. This couple stands in marked contrast to the others because of their openness, but it is a contrast partly rooted in their matching, rather unconventional backgrounds.

A Definition of Affairs

We are using the term *affair* for a sexual relationship between people who are not married to each other but at least one of the partners in the relationship is married to someone else. Other terminology has been used to signify the same phenomenon, including *infidelity* and *adultery*. Both of these terms carry a moral judgment: adultery alludes to the biblical injunction against it; infidelity means unfaithful, since an infidel is one who breaks faith and a moral commitment.

The word *affair* does not carry these moralistic overtones, but it does perhaps imply something frivolous. The difficulty of finding the appropriate terminology is related to both the difficult feelings aroused by the phenomenon and the variations in the phenomenon itself. Some affairs are frivolous, unimportant in the larger scheme of the participants' lives, and sometimes short-lived—a "best-forgotten few hours in a long life," as one person said in an interview. Others are serious, sometimes even life-changing, and sometimes virtually life-long. Some are like parallel marriages, others intermittently important, others almost forgotten. Can a single word, or indeed a single concept, encompass all of these?

Just as there has been little agreement about terminology on the subject, there has also been little consensus about how best to categorize these various relationships. Most current attempts have begun with the view that an affair points up something lacking in a marriage. Frank Pittman, in *Private Lies*, calls affairs adultery and expounds the view that the adulterer is acting "sick." The sickness that infects a marriage consequently needs treatment—therapy—to "cure" it. He says affairs can be one of three kinds. They might be *accidental* ("it just happened"). They might be of the *philandering* kind that occur mostly in men, who in Pittman's description "depersonalize both the woman at home and the woman in bed at the moment." When this kind of affair occurs, he says, there is little relationship with the wife in marital sex and in the sex outside. Affairs may be *romantic*. These affairs involve love or its near equivalent and compete with feelings for one's spouse. Affairs can also be *marital arrangements*: affairs within open marriages in which sex outside is acceptable. Pittman's views are strong and guided by a fierce moral conviction. Affairs are wrong. Monogamous marriage is healthy. His classifications are forged by this moral severity and consequently describe too narrowly the variety of affairs that exist.

Emily Brown, in her book for therapists who deal with affairs, has a different classification: There is the *out-the-door* affair in which the partner having the affair is really trying to end the marriage, the *sexual addict* affair in which sexual commitment to one person poses a never-ending problem for this type of person; and the *conflict avoiding* affair and the *intimacy avoiding* affair, both of which divert energy from the marriage (either away from conflict resolution or from the achievement of intimacy). Again, Brown takes a strong if less than moralistic view. For her, affairs are always a symptom of something amiss in a marriage and therefore a good diagnostic aid to what must be done to save it, if possible.

Affairs, Brown holds, carry a message. The message may be about the marriage itself, or it may be about what the person having the affair needs or wants to get but is not getting from the marriage. Or it can be about what a person is diverting from the marriage. For instance, in the *conflict avoiding* affair a woman who is very angry with her husband for not being loving enough may take up with someone else. She thus avoids venting her anger at her spouse both by pouring energy into an affair and also by getting attention elsewhere. Her affair cures her of feeling unnoticed and may thus diminish her anger. For Brown, affairs, though they may benefit the individual, as witness this hypothetical woman, cannot ever help a marriage. For marriages, affairs are not only bad news but also represent the worm in the apple. Brown's view—that marriage ought to be monogamous because spouses and not other lovers ought to be able to give each other sufficient emotional and sexual sustenance to avoid affairs—limits her categorization of them. In her classification, affairs are always negative comments on marriages.

In her book on affairs, Annette Lawson classifies them as either *romantic* (that is, an affair that encroaches on the romantic ideals which marriage is suppposed to embody) or those that enact the *myth of me* (that is, an affair that signifies the participant has chosen self-actualization over the growth of the marital relationship). Lawson does not take a position on the morality or healthiness of affairs; hers is a sociological analysis of what motivates people to have them. But her classification leaves out the differences men and women bring to their affairs as well as the psychological reasons people have them. Her classification also avoids a central issue in affairs: whether they are secret or open.

We have found that people classify their affairs in other ways, too. In interviews we found that they do so according to the importance of and satisfaction brought from affairs in two specific areas: their emotions and the impact of affairs on them sexually. They also add the category of time—both the duration of the affair and the amount of time spent together during it.

In terms of the emotional impact of affairs, people think of affairs along a continuum, from casual to serious. In addition, they can tell whether or not they considered themselves to have been in love with their affair partner, whether or not they liked him or her, and whether or not the emotions kindled by this partner posed a real threat to their marriage. In Annie's affair with the man on her self-awareness vacation there was little emotional attachment, and none after the affair ended, while Sam's attachment to Ellen was deep, intense, and posed a real threat to his marriage. Christina's affair felt threatening to her marriage only at its end, although she was in love with her partner. And in Ursula's there was affection but not love, and no threat to her marriage.

Another way people classify their affairs is that of time. This is usually not unrelated to the one of emotion, although that relationship is not always simple. A casual affair is often a brief one or a one-night stand. Indeed, pointing out the briefness of an affair can become a strategy for minimizing its effects: "It was very brief" or "It was just a one-night stand." This often comforts the spouse because time stolen from the marriage is minimal, and it implies the investment in the affair was insignificant. Yet sometimes brief affairs can be very traumatic. Diana, a mother of two in her early thirties who was married for twelve years, had a brief affair with her tennis instructor. Two years later she has still not recovered. The affair revealed to her that sex and romance can be deeper and more intense than she had imagined; she wants them both now and mourns their absence. Similarly, a long-term affair need not be emotionally important. Nick, a middle-aged academic with three sons, has had a recurring affair, conducted once a year over the course of about ten years, with a foreign colleague. His is an intermittent long-term affair that is of modest emotional significance. However, some long-term affairs become a bit like alternative marriages, as we shall see with Cathy and Bruce. These have built-in rules, habits, and customs like marriages themselves. If both partners have families and jobs, long-term affairs especially need to be well-governed by rules and habits. For example, "We meet Friday afternoons, except if the children are sick," "I phone you at 9:30 on Wednesday, unless there is an emergency or my husband is around, in which case we will wait until your phone call to me on Thursday afternoon, and so forth." In busy lives with potentially conflicting commitments there is not much room for unpredictability if an affair as well as a marriage are to endure over time. Of course, a long-term affair is often serious, demanding time, attention, and a commit-ment to the considerable energy it takes to maintain it.

In terms of the sexual dimension, people rate not only the degree of satisfaction and excitement an affair afforded but also whether or not they felt they had learned something about them-selves sexually and how central the sexual element was to the affair. Annie, whose first affair was with someone she met at an evening class, knew that sex was the central attraction in this one, for it con-firmed both her sexiness and her appetite. Ursula felt that sex was not as satisfactory with Sean as with her husband David, yet because she was an "adulteress" she grew sexier with David. In that sense sex was important in her affair but not because she was enor-mously attracted to her lover.

Jacqueline, a dance instructor, had an affair with a man who was both her friend and her husband's. She says that the affair enhanced marital sex. She and her affair partner became sexually involved (although no penetration ever occurred) during a theater production in which they were both working. They spent hours together, joined by their shared creative work. Her partner's passion for her was profound, and she was heady with it. Like Ursula, she was not transported by the actual sex, but being desired made her sexier with her husband.

Similarly, Neil, an academic, married to Marie for seventeen years, had numerous affairs. One was with his doctor. "Sex with Marie is great," he said. But when he talked about seducing his doc-tor, his eyes lit up. While sex with Marie might be great, it can never be illicit, a seduction electrified by the forbidden. While defined essentially as sexual relationships, sex may or may not be the most satisfactory or important element in an affair. It is the cen-tral element in defining an affair because once a relationship becomes sexual, a forbidden line has been crossed.

These classifications begin to indicate some ways we can start to manage or understand the mass of details surrounding affairs. But they do leave out a lot of the substance—particularly the substance of what we call the gender divide—as well as the constructions, or models, of marriage in which people live and which inform their experience of affairs, other predisposing factors that precede affairs and may make some people vulnerable to them, and finally the all-important divide of whether or not an affair is secret. If these issues are not analyzed when it comes to affairs, the classifications become much too narrow.

Affairs: Posing a Challenge

Let us return to the men and women who opened this chapter. If these were our neighbors, friends, or colleagues at work, why would we be shocked by their stories?

Affairs implicitly pose a challenge to our prevailing beliefs about marriage. As such, they shake our complacency. For a moment we have to think, "Could this be me?" or "Why not me?" They further challenge our ideas about marriage being a partnership in which we own or possess our spouse, an implicit code by which most marriages live: "*My* wife/*my* husband." Clearly, if a spouse can go to bed with someone else, that spouse is not possessed by the other. As we will discuss in chapter 4, this possessiveness is particularly true for husbands, since modern Western marriage grew out of a patriarchy in which families, including wives, belonged to husbands. And the still strong double standard growing out of that patriarchy makes having affairs a greater transgression for women than for men. Affairs also contradict the very vows that supposedly bind most marriages: thou shalt forsake all others, in sickness and in health, till death us do part.

But they are unsettling in other ways. We are not talking about platonic friendships between men and women, business partnerships, nonsexual social relationships between the sexes. We are talking about sexual activities shared between them, with degrees and varieties of feelings attached. We are calling attention to the sexual joining of men and women in heterosexual affairs. This will always be titillating. We have rules for sex that try to reduce the titillation: in the marital bed only, please. These rules merely reduce but never quite remove it. Perhaps there is always something fundamentally unsettling about men and women joining so intimately, stemming from the gender divide that itself suggests they can never be really joined. The gender divide, existing from the outset, shapes fundamentally different beings, as we shall discuss in chapters 2 and 3. Heterosexual affairs, being about heterosexual sex, may disturb, in part because they simultaneously indicate the always present gender divide, yet they also literally destroy it through sexual union. Homosexual affairs disturb for other reasons, and we shall turn to these in a moment. But the shock value of heterosexual affairs is inescapable partly because they disturb both social conventions and private assumptions and partly also because they are about that mysterious phenomenon: heterosexual sex.

What We Are Not Looking at in This Book

This book focuses on heterosexual affairs. From what we have said up to now it should be clear that heterosexual affairs have a different character from homosexual ones. For one thing, married people who have homosexual affairs may have them at least in part for different reasons. They may prefer to have sex with members of their own sex and sexual frustration in marriage can never be remedied within it. Or if bisexual they may feel only partly sexually alive if they are only having sex with members of the opposite sex. Homosexual affairs may seem less competitive than heterosexual ones to those having them (but not necessarily to their spouses). That is, sexual relationships with members of one's own sex may feel so different that it may be easier to believe that they exist parallel to, rather than in conflict with, marriages. In addition, people impose secrecy in homosexual affairs for special reasons. Most married people who have homosexual affairs prefer to be seen publicly as heterosexual. Thus secrecy about homosexual affairs carries additional urgency. And the repercussions upon discovery of secret homosexuality, such as disgrace, stigma, deeper shock, and the need to recast the affair person's identity, are additional to any in a heterosexual affair.

Similarly, we are not including visits to prostitutes as affairs. In these, the reasons sex is entered into is different. There is a clear exchange, money for sex. No one easily nurtures other agendas. These are still sexual encounters outside marriage, admittedly, but even proverbial one-night stands normally include something more personal. They are usually preceded by some conversation in which there is some appeal on the part of both participants to be viewed as more than their genitals. These other desires and agendas can exist with prostitution, of course, but they are not necessary or expected. The discovery of secret one-night stands has the potential of unsettling the marital status quo in a way that prostitute visits do not. The spouse can realistically wonder if there was or could have been something more—affection or desire for more contact, for instance. This is not true of prostitute visits (although if a man visits the same prostitute a number of times, the likelihood of some feeling growing for that woman may increase), and a spouse may therefore feel more emotionally secure. Indeed, prostitute visits currently pose a different sort of threat: the increased risk of contracting AIDS or other sexually transmitted diseases. They also often incur suspicions that one's spouse might not be sexually normal (and so is compelled to visit prostitutes for kinky or other disturbing practices). For these reasons they can and often do disturb marriages profoundly. But they can be more easily dismissed as "just for sex."

Also, in this book we are discussing only affairs that are sexual. Some people consider it an affair when the involvement is emotional but not sexual. Most sexual affairs include some form of emotional involvement, even if minimal in duration and importance. The fact that they are sexual makes them different.

What is problematic about our definition is the difficulty in defining what is sexual. Many people define it as an affair when penetration takes place. Since intercourse is the marital act, perhaps people give themselves the benefit of the doubt. We think using "penetration" as the only criterion is sticking to the letter, rather than the spirit of an affair. Sex without intercourse is one way of accommodating the desire for an affair and the notion that one is still faithful, like a virgin outside of marriage. It is not clear whether spouses would agree. Some may want to hear that intercourse did not actually take place in order to forgive.

The story of Paul and Emily underscores this point. Paul and Emily had an open marriage, but their contract excluded Paul's having affairs while Emily was pregnant or breast-feeding. After the birth of their second child, Paul found himself irresistibly drawn to

Stephanie, a colleague at work. He confessed this to Emily, hoping to renegotiate their agreement, but she refused. His attraction to Stephanie did not wane, and they began to meet. Eventually they became sexually involved, and if one uses Kinsey's measure, the number of orgasms achieved, they were very active sexually, and they certainly fit the definition. But penetration never occurred. For Paul this meant that he was honoring his marital agreement, and he therefore did not define what he and Stephanie were doing as having an affair. We would define Paul and Stephanie's relationship as an affair. When there is substantial sexual involvement, and especially genital contact, it constitutes an affair for us.

Affairs and AIDS

Affairs mean an increased risk of contracting the HIV virus. The ultimate safe sex is monogamy. In interviews for this book only two people spontaneously mentioned AIDS. One said that in recent years he has not had any casual affairs because of the risk. The other, in an affair with a bisexual man, said that this man had recently had an HIV test that was negative, so she felt safe sleeping with him. Most had not been promiscuous and considered themselves to be in low-risk groups, and so they did not take precautions to avoid any sexually transmitted diseases.

It is our impression, and most of the current research has shown, that people who are not homosexual, bisexual, or intravenous drug users still do not consider HIV infection a risk they are running, especially if they do not have many sexual partners. It is possible that there may be less activity at the more casual end of the affair spectrum, but people do seem to be continuing to have affairs. Certainly affairs are now riskier than before. And the secrecy rests on even shakier ground. If an affair partner turns out to be HIV-positive and one contracts the virus, there is nothing defensible about keeping the affair secret anymore. Yet even so, the irresistibility of affairs is undeniable for enormous numbers of people.

This irresistibility, the fact that even despite the specter of AIDS people are drawn in possibly increasing numbers to sexual liaisons outside of marriage, is what compels us to dissect affairs. What is it about them that is so attractive? What are they like for men and women? How do some marriages accommodate them while others do not? *Why* affairs? And *what*, indeed, are they about? We propose to address these issues in this book.

2

Men's Love/
Women's Love

Woman wants monogamy;
Man delights in novelty.
Love is woman's moon and sun;
Man has other forms of fun.
Woman lives but in her lord;
Count to ten, and man is bored.
With this the gist and sum of it,
What earthly good can come of it?

Dorothy Parker, *Not So Deep as a Well* (1937)

OTH MEN AND WOMEN WANT TO FALL IN LOVE AND BE IN love. But women say it more often. Until recently a girl's upbringing concentrated on finding a man to marry and then bearing his children. Even though this is less true now, died-in-the-wool career women still feel incomplete when not in an intimate relationship. In contrast, men view relationships as extra to themselves, something desirable added. As one therapy patient said: "Of course I want to be in love, but I've got this Ph.D. to do. My girlfriend wants attention, love, declarations of passion—I don't have the time right now." Both in interviews for this book and in therapy sessions, men have claimed that first and foremost they are their careers. Thereafter they are husbands, fathers, sons, and friends. In contrast, in similar interviews, more women defined themselves first as mothers, wives, and friends, and they are *also* career women.

While men crave love, they express it differently. For example, for men bereavement over a particular woman is understandable—for example, when a love affair ends or a wife dies—but longing for some undefined woman is not; a man crying over his loneliness is undignified. Yet a "real woman" is defined in part by intimacy with another: she is unfinished on her own. Recently we saw an article by a divorced career woman in a popular magazine. While still championing the importance of self-reliance, she realized she functions at half-mast without a man. This was manifestly a woman's testimony. The same article by a man would have been about missing companionship or yearning for sex, not bemoaning his incompleteness because he was alone.

So, while both men and women want to be in love, they seem to be after different things. Men want women to be separate yet bring pleasure, interest, enjoyment, and warmth. Understandably, women share these wants, but they also seek completion through relationships. This difference emerges even when women act less like traditional women and more like traditional men, segmenting or setting boundaries to their sexual involvements (as we will discuss in chapter 5). Even then women are thinking both about the whole complicated web of others involved directly and indirectly in their affairs and also about how having such a relationship reflects on them. They continue to define themselves through their attachments to others. Men do not. In keeping with their clearer boundaries, men talk about things done together, what each partner does for the other in the affair, or what each spouse gets out of a marriage. The language they use to describe love is earthbound and practical.

The story of gender differences in love is complex. To understand it we must look at the ways in which tendencies toward connectedness in girls and separateness in boys develop. From the earliest years the needs in adult romantic relationships have been shaped differently for men and women.

The Gender Divide

Gender is perhaps the most important single definer of how we experience and view the world. From the beginning gender plays a major role in how we related to our mothers—whether we (as a daughter) identified with her or (as a son) felt different. Gender is also at the root of male/female differences in relationships in another way. It is a basic feature of all our experience. Because of gender a person responds to the world (including parent or caregiver) in particular ways. In a sense we can say that there are two worlds: one seen from the perspective of a girl and one seen from the perspective of a boy. We become socialized *as* girls or boys. We then behave as boys *or* girls, and the world (including our parents and caregivers) responds to us accordingly. Thus we live as one or the other gender in a world that is itself split by this same divide.

Most people recognize that men and women differ in their experience of courtship, marriage, friendship, and love. In affairs, too, they behave differently. They experience different feelings. They have different needs and expectations. In this chapter we will look at how these differences begin—when we are small babies and later growing children. We are going to look at the development of feelings and emotions in men and women—not at sexuality, which we will examine in the next chapter. Emotions and sexual behavior *are* separate—although they are usually experienced as inextricably entangled.

The setting for our discussion is, of course, the world of the West—of an industrialized, advanced society. Men, women, and affairs would look quite different in the context, say, of tribal Africa or communist China. But we are looking specifically at couples interviewed in America and Britain, couples affected by the expectations of the society they live in. But even within their societies there will be an enormous range of behavior.

For example, in our society women are largely responsible for taking care of the children. If a man becomes the primary caretaker (particularly from the outset), the children will grow up with different sorts of personalities from those brought up by women. Boys brought up primarily by nurturing men should be more able to be emotional and close with others than boys brought up primarily by women. Another variant is how different families approach sex. Some families are prudish about sex and others are relaxed. Still others depart completely from what society defines as normal and permissible sexual behavior.

At thirty-one, Bob, a married truck driver with two young sons, was arrested for molesting young girls. In his family all four children had been sexually abused by one or both parents as well as by their grandfather. At puberty Bob began to sleep regularly with his mother after his father left home, taking his two sisters. Bob's conception of what constitutes appropriate sexual behavior developed abnormally, if sensibly, within the context of his family's practices. This may be an extreme example, but it illustrates two points. First, each family varies in its approach to sex. Second, the family in which we are raised plays a critical role in shaping our ideas about sexuality and about how relationships are formed.

Different cultures or subcultures have varying definitions about what signals sex. Olivia, a twenty-year-old Englishwoman, had gone on a camping expedition with a mixed group from Britain and a Muslim country. She was raped by one of the Muslim boys when, exhausted after a day's climbing, she stretched out on a camp bed while alone in a room with him. In his culture if a woman lies on a bed in a room alone with a man, it is a sexual invitation. In Olivia's culture the group camaraderie would have canceled out sexual overtones, making hers an innocent gesture.

Developing as Girls or Boys

The dilemma of monogamy versus affairs in marriage stems in large part from the transposition of the exclusivity of our very first love to our expectations of all the rest of our loves. Our next love, of course, most commonly develops during adolescence. The moon-June-honeymoon falling-in-love style of this first adolescent romantic love serves to reinforce those patterns set in infancy. Women and men are different, but in one critical way they are the same.

They both want love, and they both think exclusivity and love go together since they are both reared in similarly intense mother-and-child pairs. The similarity stops there. We now look at how this first one-to-one exclusive love develops for boys and girls.

In order to form a close relationship we need to have a sense of ourselves as individuals. For that we need a sense of self. Newborns do not have this. They respond to what is done to them. For example, they may smile in response to a soft familiar voice, but they do not have a sense of themselves as distinct entities. This comes only through exchanges with those around them, usually parents, possibly in conjunction with brothers and sisters. For the great majority of infants in our society the most important person who interacts with the infant is the mother. A sense of self is developed in social interaction throughout life. Whoever looks after us when we are babies is crucial to our developing a sense of ourselves. In our society this is usually the mother; more to the point, it is usually a female.

The fact that the caregiver is female has an effect on both the child's sense of self and on the way he or she relates to others. This stems from the fact that mothers—or the female caregivers—treat boy babies differently from the way they treat girls. After a while babies also begin to respond differently to female, rather than male, caregivers. The most significant contributor to this difference, as others before us have also said, is that, sharing gender, a mother identifies with a girl baby and feels separate from a boy.

We think about ourselves in terms of our gender—we are, before we are anything else, men or women. Gender, in turn, is defined for us by our society. Our gender informs our experience of the world and the world's experience of us. Research observations made of newborn babies and their parents' handling of them reinforce the point that a mother will and can normally identify with a girl baby in a way she will not and cannot with a boy. Studies have shown that both parents seem to handle newborn boy babies more roughly than newborn girls. They also talk more to girls than to boys. What is interesting about these findings is not only the fact that they indicate the strength of societal expectations of boys and girls but they also illustrate the handing down from women to women and men to men of the way they think about themselves.

Their own gender experience is part of what is being seen in these parents' treatment of their newborn children.

This gender-related caregiving has a profound effect on creating male/female differences in both relationships and people's experience of themselves. The important point here is that these then become propensities that differentiate the way the sexes behave in adult relationships. As we shall describe later when we examine the experience of affairs for men and women, this tendency to merge or to be separate is central to how men and women think about and report their affairs.

Female Connectedness/Male Separateness

When a baby is born, it is dependent and unaware. In any way we can define a "self," the baby has no sense of it. It feels no distinction between what is itself and what is other. As it begins to get a sense of differentiation of itself, other people, and the world, the "other" is usually a mother. At first the baby does not know what it is to be apart. It is as if there is no separation between baby and mother; each merges into the other. As the baby matures, increasing the range of things it does, it begins to be aware that there is something which is itself—"baby"—and something which is mother, father, sister. Gradually the secure knowledge that the mother is there allows the baby to explore—first his or her body, then the world—all of which contributes to the baby's growing sense of self.

Part of the sense the baby develops that he or she is something separate comes from the fact that the baby's mother is not always immediately available. She cannot always be there and is not able to meet every need the baby has. The baby may feel hungry but has to wait to be fed. Or a wet diaper cannot be changed immediately. But a mother's inability to meet each need perfectly actually helps stimulate her baby's sense of separateness and hence its self-development. With a developing sense of self comes something like love for the mother. Until then, just as he cannot feel a sense of self, the baby cannot feel love. Our sense of self always develops within a relationship from birth onward. In order to love someone else, we must feel a sense of self, someone who is separate. There cannot be adult relationships without a sense of self.

This sense of separation, central to developing a sense of self, is what is most keenly different between boys and girls and then between men and women. As we have said, the typical child care arrangements of our society produce a mother-daughter bond of empathy or identification and a mother-son division from the start.

When Beth was thirteen she and her mother, Angie, began to have serious arguments. Until that time they had had a warm, close relationship. But at twelve Beth discovered boys. Her mother deeply disapproved. The previous harmony between them gave way to acrimonious arguments. "You're going to end up just like the rest of them—ordinary, boy crazy. When was the last time you read a book?" Angie would shout at Beth. Angie hated the fact that her daughter, with whom she had identified as a younger child, was becoming interested in boys at an earlier age than Angie had and was also demonstrating behavior that embarrassed and appalled her. Angie had been a late developer and a good student. Much of her own self-esteem had come from her success as a student and then in the career that she gave up when she had children. Hers was a traditional marriage; her husband worked and she looked after their two children. Her little girl, Beth, was a bright, inventive child who shone in school. The identification between them was strengthened by similar interests and temperament. Angie felt she was a good mother and understood her daughter. A critical difference emerged in adolescence: Beth was much prettier and matured earlier than her mother. Angie felt their close and intuitive bond weakening. She cringed as she watched Beth become an accomplished flirt. Remembering her own loss of dignity as she tried but failed to gain boys' attention made it impossible for Angie to let her own daughter learn her own lessons and make her own mistakes. Increasingly, her diminishing identification with her daughter led Angie to feel she was a failure as a mother. But identification for this pair had meant that one had merged too fully with the other. Angie could not see her daughter for the woman she was becoming.

Angie also had a son, Michael. Although they had difficulty when he reached adolescence, she gave him far greater latitude. Betrayal wasn't involved when his interests and tastes developed in what she considered foreign ways. In a sense he had been foreign to her from the start. When, at eight, Michael became a football player and was desperate to be the best in his class, she identified with his wanting to be the best and with his disappointment at being not quite good enough. But because the world of boys, their interests and responses, is so different from the world of girls, she did not mistake his experience for hers. This gave Michael a greater degree of freedom from her anxiety than his sister. Angie was left to conclude that she was a better mother to Michael than to Beth, despite identifying so closely with her daughter.

Beth's and Michael's experiences with the same mother were different in large part because of their gender. So merged with Angie was Beth that she bought Angie's values—and judgment on her— almost completely. The fact that she chose to go on a date rather than read a novel seemed to confirm that she was going to be "ordinary" and that she would lose her mother's respect and approval. So merged was she with her mother that she felt terrible because of her difference and independence. But Michael's experience was different. When his mother overempathized, he cut her off, even as a young boy. Averting his face became his characteristic nonverbal message to his mother; it said: "Enough. Don't get so close. Let me be." And she did because he already was different from her.

Even in less traditional, more egalitarian marriages mothers take ultimate responsibility for most duties attached to children, except perhaps for financial provision. And if the mother works, child care is then usually assumed not by the father or some other male but by another woman, whether nanny, babysitter, grandmother, or another female relative. When the children go off to school, especially in the early years, they go off to the care of other women. Teachers in nursery and primary schools are not usually men. So it is not overstating things to say that the child-care arrangements of our society are still overwhelmingly the province of women. Babies and young children spend most of their time in female company.

Lynn, a forty-year-old, twice-married psychologist and mother of three who has had a difficult and distant relationship with her mother, speaks of resenting her less gifted, more ordinary brother because of his easy relationship with her: "I actually had her standing there in front of me," she said recently in an interview, "looking at me and saying, 'I don't know where you came from!' And that's just how I feel. I went into psychology, I'm sure, to find out how it could happen that I could be so different from her. Meanwhile, she and my brother are just the same—they'd be happy sitting at home watching the same T.V. shows together for the rest of their lives. They don't know what I'm talking about." There is little sympathy between these two women, and their experiences are extremely different yet nothing can change the fact that gender binds mother and daughter together. Mothers "know" what their girl babies are like or will be like, although they may often get it wrong. They have learned what they think their boy babies are like or will be like. And they treat each, from the first, differently. Fathers do this, too; a father's influence is not trivial, and indeed he acts as a reinforcer.

Children do indeed have to learn to share their mothers with another grown-up—usually the father, in most family arrangements. Even in single-parent families, children have to learn the inevitable lesson of sharing. At the same time they must confront the notion of their limited power compared to the grown-up challenger in this battle. The father is a powerful person, both in relation to the child and also in comparison with the mother. Most children will perceive, at quite a young age, that there is a real power difference between men and women. Or, as one three-year-old put it, "Daddy's the boss of the money. Mommy's the boss of the dirt." This father also often adores his little girl or boy, so there is indeed immediately something "in it" for these children to accommodate this powerful "other" in the triangle. In other words, most children, partly because they have to and partly because they want to, make the accommodation. This is the process that Freud was the first to describe, the one he called the resolution of the Oedipal "crisis." But it is a different process, with different results, for boys and girls.

For girls, this first important relationship with Daddy—with someone of the opposite sex—carries sexual overtones. Again, this is specific to our Western culture. Our popular icon of a sexy woman is one with girlish—even infantile—characteristics: we find something sexual in little girls. Marilyn Monroe's voice was girlish. Yet icons of male sexuality have no suggestion of babyishness: John Wayne's shoulders bore large and heavy burdens. This is not to imply any overt sexuality in father-daughter relationships. However, it is saying that from the beginning we unconsciously sexualize male-to-female relationships. Since little boys—with piping voices and narrow shoulders—bear no resemblance to sexy adult men from the outset, that element is absent in boys' first female-to-male relationship. Because, furthermore, little girls learn to take a submissive role in this first relationship with a man, the father-daughter relationship has the quality of providing a model for later heterosexual relationships; this is not true of the mother-son one.

The patterning of later heterosexual relationships on those of fathers and daughters that begins so early is strikingly emphasized by findings in studies of the effects of divorce on children. When divorce results in daughters losing contact with their fathers, these girls may do poorly in their later relationships with men. They are more likely to have negative views of men and may also fail to make lasting and trusting heterosexual relationships.

The underlying sexuality of the father-daughter relationship is ironically highlighted at the girl's adolescence when many warm and affectionate father-daughter relationships are cut off and become cold just when girls become sexual beings. This is not usually conscious or deliberate. It stems partly from awkwardness: how does a cuddle not now seem sexual? In contrast, this is not a dilemma for mothers and sons. Instead, for them the problem is how does a cuddle not seem childish? It also can stem from a father's often unconscious sexual jealousy. When Alan went on a school trip with his fourteen-year-old daughter, he returned home angry and critical of her. He confessed to his wife that he thought their daughter was probably unhappy with him during the trip since he had been temperamental and short-tempered. The evidence of her unhappiness with him came from his observation that she had spent most of her time on the trip with Brian, "an obnoxious boy." Unaware of the conversation between her parents, their daughter also confided in her mother, but her report was all about Brian, the "gorgeous boy" who had paid her a lot of attention.

The emotional merging of mother and daughter is not threatened by the formation of a strong bond between father and daughter. Their relationship—the rehearsal for a later boy-girl relationship—is so different from the mother-daughter bond that they coexist comfortably. In contrast, fathers help effect a further separation, beyond the one given by their difference in gender, between mothers and sons. Sons identify with fathers; fathers are able to attract these identifications largely because they are seen as more powerful than mothers. In this stage of development in early childhood, which marks something of a separation from the mother for both sexes, girls stay more connected to their mothers than boys, who begin to separate more.

Connectedness and Girls' Early Development

A quality often used to describe good mothering is empathy. It entails close identification. A responsive mother is an empathic one: she can "read" her baby—identify with it. For example, it is often said that every mother knows her baby's cry. To someone who isn't listening for his or her own baby's cry, any cry sounds like any other. But to a mother her baby's is unique. Moreover, she can usually tell what *kind* of cry it is—tiredness, pain, hunger, the need for contact. Mothers can *feel* these cries, in a way, in order to read them and respond to them.

This kind of empathic identification, which has an intuitive base, is clearly something that will be fostered in little girls because of the very closeness of their relationship with the mother. It will be reinforced daily within the mother-child relationship. Girls thus have more advantageous conditions for developing this capacity for close and intimate relationships from the outset. The mother-daughter bond promotes both an expectation that there will be connections between people and a way of defining oneself in relation to others: watching for their response to you, appraising their effect on you, and vice-versa. This propensity to assess and experience the world in this way is both a gift and a liability for women, as we shall see.

A mother's identifying too closely with her infant daughter can become a problem. Identification with a girl baby can easily tip over into *over*identification, actually *denying* the baby daughter's separateness or her sense of self. For instance, Jackie, a very young mother from a very deprived background, during which she experienced successive abandonments by her own mother, brought her six-month-old daughter for an appointment with a researcher. The baby cried on and off for the half hour Jackie sat in the waiting room. Jackie did not hold her or rock her or try to feed her. Only occasionally did she soothe her child by rocking the carriage. When the researcher finally arrived, she picked up the baby and her cries lessened. "She's only trying to get attention," Jackie said offhandedly as the trio entered the research office. "My mom says I was just the same. She says it just spoils kids to pick them up."

Overprotection can be born of the same thing. The opening scene of *Terms of Endearment* shows Shirley MacLaine tiptoeing into her infant daughter's bedroom, ostensibly to check on her. More important than making a check on her daughter's well-being, she goes to the room for herself: for reassurance that her child is still breathing. The visit also reassures her that she is necessary; she settles her now-awake baby's cries. Presumably this mother thinks that she is responding to her daughter, "reading" her daughter's needs but actually conflating them with her own.

These two cases exemplify a clear lack of empathy: the mother's overidentification obscures the baby's actual needs with the mother's misread ones. Instead she reads what hers would be or have been said to be (or what hers were or still are, as the mother relives and perhaps rewrites her own childhood history). Thus, because of overconnectedness, there is actually a lack of real empathy.

This connectedness, merging, or identification breeds in girls both the virtues of being able to empathize with others more easily and the problems of fuzzier boundaries. Girls and women are less clear where the "me" starts and ends. They consequently have more difficulty in knowing what might be good for them as opposed to others (not to mention in *asking for* what would be good for them). The difference in how women and men conduct their relationships can thus be seen to emanate from these earliest times.

Simon and Susie were married for nine years when Simon had a secret affair. Susie began her career training under Simon. They fell in love, moved in together, and eventually married. For eight years they lived and worked together every day, day in, day out.

Their intense relationship was also rocky: Susie often initiated arguments by complaining that she felt neglected, unappreciated, and unnoticed. About a year into their relationship Simon began working long, hard hours, sometimes returning to their shared office after dinner and not returning until Susie was asleep. Susie wanted more of Simon, Simon wanted less. For Susie the merging she experienced, the looseness of their boundaries even down to the working space they shared, comforted her and felt natural. For Simon it felt too close, too merged. He wanted to break away, which is what he attempted to do by having an affair that almost ended their marriage.

Separateness and Boys' Early Development

If boys tend toward difficulty in relationships, it is in the other direction and stems from too much separation or an *under*identification. For boys the task of defining a separate self is helped by the mother's perception of herself as separate. These firmer boundaries between them help to explain the basis of what research into personality preferences and achievement differences between boys and girls has reported as boys' greater ability to be single-minded and clear.

This emerges in a variety of ways, from pursuit of career to the division made more often by men between love and sex and to greater assertiveness. A mundane example of this is from accounts given by mothers of very young babies when these mothers were interviewed in a study of their first year of adjustment to the maternal role. Many mothers found it baffling that their husbands could come home from a hard day at work, sit down, and read the newspaper, often while the baby was crying. These women would be exhausted by hours of being on-call for their families, with little sleep. Their most commonly voiced complaint was "I don't have time for myself." And this was on the most basic levels—they were perplexed by how to have time "to go to the bathroom." They complained of dirty hair from not finding a space in the day in which to wash it—again because they were responding to the needs of others first. They were often amazed and baffled by their husband's ability to tune out, sit down, and relax with the paper. The more accepting of these understood the husband's need to unwind, to do something for himself. The less accepting saw it as selfish. Many felt envious. Many recognized that their husbands knew what they needed; they had clearer boundaries around the "me."

It is our belief that this quality stems from the first baby-mother relationship. The fuzzier boundaries girls experience help to make them people who consider what others feel, who react to and think about others each time they act. They act, as the developmental psychologist Carol Gilligan has described it, within a "web of relationships." That is what defines them as much as their actions themselves. "Self"—if self is in part defined by how someone characteristically acts—for women is in this way tied to others. "Self" for men is not.

The empathic identification between mother and child can promote a sense of connectedness. The problem for boy babies may be that their mothers make the mistake of *under*identifying, as they may overidentify with daughters. Since from the beginning the mother knows that there is something fundamentally different about her boy baby, the sense of connection, even merging, with one's child is unlikely to occur between them. This can mean that boys more often lack empathic identification. The result is that they may be too cut off.

Sam married a woman who was quite timid and undemanding, unintrusive and thrilled by her husband. She lacked the passion and nervous energy that marked Ellen, his lover. Sam did not feel his wife could understand much of his often murky emotional life. His mother was an intrusive, controlling woman, and he both loved and steered clear of her, while he adored his sweet-tempered father but was contemptuous of his ineffectualness. Ellen understood his complexity. In the end he left Ellen. The potential was too great that he would feel smothered. At bottom, Sam was sad and lonely at home with his low-key but adoring wife, and he missed Ellen and her devouring passion, but he was unwilling to risk being smothered by it as he almost was by his mother.

In the final section of this chapter we will explore the different approaches this kind of early development creates for men and women—and the different vulnerabilities for each—in pursuing adult romantic relationships. First we turn to further divergent pathways taken during adolescence.

Adolescence and the Widening of the Gender Gap

In adolescence boys and girls are both expected and seem inclined to sexualize relationships with the opposite sex. So in adolescence early developmental differences clearly emerge in expectations, beliefs, and behaviors in relationships.

All recent indicators show that while girls may be pursuing higher education, professional training, and careers far more than a generation ago, they still put a tremendous premium on being in a relationship. They are more likely than boys to want to marry and to marry earlier. While it is now normal for both sexes to have sexual intercourse before they marry, girls still worry about their "reputations." Even in an era of greater sexual freedom for both sexes, boys have more freedom, and there is still a double standard. This is not only a societal standard—it seems to accord with a girl's inner development. Girls want to be connected. If they are in stable relationships, they feel more secure not only in their position but also in how they define themselves.

In adolescence, as boys and girls begin to look like men and women, demands are accelerated that they begin to act like men and women as well. Adolescence is a time of apprenticeship in adult gender roles. During adolescence, as we shall see in the next chapter, the emphasis on heterosexual relationships burgeons. Differences between girls and boys in sexual behavior, imagery, and attitudes widen. It is as if by separating the sexes in this way at this time, when their bodies make it possible and inevitable that they will become sexual, we help to tantalize them by accentuating foreignness; by creating a divide we reinforce the forbiddenness of heterosexual sex.

Because of this, the sexual differences between girls and boys tend to be greatly exaggerated at adolescence, as we will discuss in the next chapter. Later they may begin to show some convergences. It is when girls are past their teenage years that they begin to have freer sexual fantasies. In Nancy Friday's work and that of others on women's sexual fantasies, women report a great range, whereas the typical adolescent girl's fantasy does not run much further than the pop songs: what is erotic is to find one person to love, kiss, cuddle, and maybe make love. "Love" is the aphrodisiac of the fantasy. However, as Barbara Ehrenreich and her co-authors point out in their book, *Remaking Love: The Feminization of Sex*, older women are now more sexually active without getting a bad reputation. Indeed, sometimes men see them as sophisticated, experienced, confident, and perhaps threatening—their sexual experience is greater and therefore possibly more powerful. In fact, the emphasis for adolescent girls on being "good," and being sexy only if one is in love and loved, is crucial in building their identities as women. It marks a girl as clearly feminine, as we will show in chapter 3: love comes first in relationships for girls; acknowledging sexual feelings apart from love comes later. But boys are first sexual; they attach "love feelings" to the sexual ones afterward.

These distinctions are very marked at adolescence but can blur as men and women develop, through experience in sex and love, as chapter 3 discusses. With greater experience as a woman may come experimentation, the attempt to stretch the boundaries of how a woman is defined. For similar reasons for boys, if there is to be a period of "sex without love," it may well occur sometime during adolescence.

Similarly at this point the emotional differences deepen as well. The main psychological task at adolescence is to discover the answer to "Who am I?" especially apart from the "who" the adolescent has been as a child in his or her family. A large part of the answer to this question lies in defining both one's sexuality and one's gender role. How are you going to be a woman or man? What will it look or feel like? Will you be much like mother or father or a bit more like Madonna or Schwarzenegger? Adolescents take first, often faltering, steps along the road toward forging their identities. As they do this, the paths of emotional development along gender lines widen. Girls pine for love; boys for sex. Girls congregate in intense pairs, boys play in groups. Girls pick apart feelings, developing highly sophisticated language for them. Boys finely hone skills, set goals, and pursue them. They let lapse any language for emotions that their mothers may have begun to inculcate in them, since their peers and fathers, with whom they now identify as men, are unlikely to be much good at talking about feelings.

Adolescents are expected to transfer their intense affections for Mommy and Daddy, developed as children, to someone else. And they expect, as part of the deal, the same intensity and exclusiveness that Mommy, particularly, delivered, especially in the beginning. Indeed, the first days, weeks, and months of falling in love are intense and exclusive; lovers are focused on and preoccupied with each other, like mother and baby in the baby's first years. So both the expectations and the demands for exclusiveness, which we see later in marriage and monogamy, are fixed in our earliest love relationship (mother and child) and are then reinforced in our next one, in adolescence.

The central problem in this is, of course, that mother-child love is not the same as either adolescent-adolescent or adult-adult love. Transposing expectations from one to the other can be dangerous. The consistent, predictable, intense preoccupation and concentration that goes on between mother and child are not possible, and probably not desirable, in a relationship between adults. And yet they are often expected.

Different Expectations: Men and Women in Love

Given men's and women's different emotional development there will be differences in their sexual relationships. Both can have problems with intimacy and both may react defensively. Both may deny the need for intimacy. Both may seek too much closeness. But women tend to do more of the latter and men more of the former. More women can be accused of emotional, if not sexual, promiscuity. Women may have too much of a tendency to connect, stemming from too-fuzzy boundaries, given that mothers may overidentify with daughters.

From underidentification men may be too cut off from others and so less able to be intimate than women. Empathy is not as easy for them. However, an alternative scenario may also emerge. Boys may grow up with unfinished business, yearning to fill the gap left by not enough intimacy early on. As men they may yield to this yearning, searching fruitlessly for an enormous, greater-than-life love. Indeed, some men may avoid the unfamiliarity of intimacy or undermine it, despite a desire for it, because they imagine intimacy is smothering.

Stuart, a graduate student in his late twenties, said, "I don't think I'm really made for love, even though I want it." Stuart had recently ended a three-year marriage after his wife began an affair and fell in love with her boss. Stuart, who spent months at a time away on field work, had preferred their relationship to be distant, punctuated by reunions. Previous relationships were also character-ized by distance—with both physical separations and emotional withdrawals. Stuart's mother, a frail, unhappy woman, had doted on him excessively until the birth of her second child; then, Stuart felt, she had "dropped" him. He experienced her as never quite understanding him but coming closer to it than his brutish, alco-holic father. He felt contempt for his younger brother (who as a grown-up lived at home with his mother). He was quite certain that his brother was homosexual, and he explained it was a result of being so identified with their mother. The family myth was that Stuart, his brother, and his mother were all alike: sensitive, literary, cultivated. The myth also alleged that it was Stuart who rejected his poor mother, while his younger brother was her rescuer. Perhaps as a result of his isolation in this family and his self-rescue from fears that his mother would swallow him up like his brother, Stuart developed a remote and independent style. He feared that whatev-er was unique to him, in comparison with his mother—including his sexuality—was in danger of being sacrificed to her. Isolation characterized him and made him very seductive to many women. They saw him as very "masculine"—independent, self-reliant, and frustratingly "hard to get."

The yearning, the unfinished business left by underidentification, may help to explain why men have a deep need for women in ways that women do not seem to need men. This is evidenced by the fact that of all people, single men do the worst on measures of mental and physical health, and men who do not remarry soon after a divorce show a comparatively high incidence of mental and physical problems. Men do remarry at faster rates than women, and this may be explained in part by the deep need men have for a secure and predictable union, complemented, of course, by the greater ability of women to offer the empathy men seek. This may be part of the phenomenon whereby women define themselves and feel themselves to be alive largely through their relationships.

Stuart's story illustrates that in men the need for intimate connection is often a denied one: men do not slaver after romantic love the way women do. It is not all right for boys to pine for love the way it is for girls. We cannot conceive of an anorexic, lovelorn male, yet girls reach such a state so frequently that it becomes difficult to always take notice. It is not macho to be girl crazy, but we smile at a gaggle of teenage girls going three times in one week to see a film that features their favorite (male) film star. This is not to say that women may not also show *pathology* in the same way—running from relationships that are too intimate, particularly if they have been smothered by their mothers or possibly their fathers (which is especially true in cases where women run from men who are too powerful). It is much more unusual for women to be isolates, though, because they define themselves through relationships more than men do. Women may suffer because they depend too much for their identity on an intimate connection.

Margaret, an attractive, upper-middle-class woman of fifty-five who was the wife of a successful business executive, came into psychotherapy because she had made a suicide attempt. Her husband had walked out after thirty-three years, two children, and one recent grandchild. Margaret's mother died when Margaret was sixteen. She had been close to her mother and identified strongly with her. She had known her somewhat older future husband, a friend of the family, all her life. Soon after her mother's death, they fell in love and became engaged, marrying when Margaret was eighteen.

She was the "perfect wife"—so perfect, in fact, that she felt herself to be nothing else. They shared everything, but on closer analysis this meant that Margaret had gone along with everything her husband wanted. His peripatetic business life meant she had literally dragged all over the world after him. She was serenely happy doing this. She loved dressing up as the business executive's wife, being introduced as "Mrs. Watson." She loved the power she saw emanating from him; it gave her an illusion of her own power. She loved the hotels, the golf club, the dances, and the restaurants, and she loved "giving him his two children and his beautiful home." His pride in her made her day. She looked forward to his approaching retirement so they could do even more things together. In contrast, with this prospect ahead of him, he fled. The story is not unusual, but it could only be a woman's.

The different pathways of emotional development find their counterpart in sexual development. Not only are men and women primed to want, think about, and experience emotional relationships differently, but their sexuality is forged in markedly different ways as well. The formation of their sexual needs, experiences, attitudes, and imagery is a feature of the gender divide that separates men and women in their experience of affairs, and we will discuss this formation in chapter 3.

3

Women and Men Together

Sexual intercourse began
In 1963
(which was rather late for me)
Between the end of the Chatterley ban
And the Beatles' first L.P.

Up till then there'd only been
A sort of bargaining,
A wrangle for a ring,
A shame that started at sixteen
And spread to everything.

Then all at once the quarrel sank;
Everyone felt the same,
And every life became
A brilliant breaking of the bank,
A quite unloseable game.

So life was never better than
In 1963
(though too late for me)—
Between the end of the Chatterley ban
And the Beatles' first L.P.

Philip Larkin, "Annus Mirabilis"

There is an apocryphal story that serves to illustrate one of the basic problems with our unquestioned expectation of monogamy in modern marriage. It is one that gives the name to a phenomenon called the "Coolidge Effect" and is supposedly about President Calvin Coolidge and his wife. President and Mrs. Coolidge, visiting a government farm, were taken on separate tours. Looking at a rooster, Mrs. Coolidge inquired if it could mate more than once a day. When she was told it could, she asked that the information be passed to the President. When the President reached the rooster's enclosure and was told about its sexual performance, he asked whether the same hen was involved each time. When he was told it was a different hen, he paused, looked thoughtful, and then said, "Please tell that to Mrs. Coolidge."

"He's gotten fat. Every time he orders a dessert when we go out, I can feel my toes curl and my heart sink, and I turn right off him. It's such a shame. I just can't drool over him the way I used to, and what's really awful is that we used to have such a good sex life," said Mary, who was dejected about sex in a marriage that has lasted twenty-three years. This same woman, interviewed a few years ago about her affair with one of her husband's friends, was at pains to tell us that her sex life with her husband was even better than hers with her affair partner. Now she imagined her former lover's body when she was in bed with her husband, whose body has, as she complained, gone flabby and soft. Sex is at a standstill for them now, for the first time in their married life.

Neil, married for thirteen years to his childhood sweetheart, talked about how sex in affairs was exciting because it was new and forbidden, and the thrill of seduction made it special. In the same conversation he reported that sex with his wife was "great. We still make love three, four times a week, and she is just terrific. We've been married so long, we can do anything together."

On the other hand, people who are married a long time sometimes stop thinking of things to do together and just get on with doing the same: "It's like, first we stroke, then we kiss, then his hand moves here and mine goes over there, and I'm thinking 'and next comes this' as soon as he does A or I do B. Not very erotic. But I come just about every time. We've learned *how* to get off, but it's not exactly something I can't wait to do." This from Alice, married seventeen years, who has never had an affair yet thinks about it constantly.

In our own species the Coolidge Effect is not simply a matter of doing the same thing with different partners but, as many couples discover, doing somewhat different things with the same partner. Indeed, couples who create a varied and developing sexual relationship are likely to maintain an interest in sex and a high frequency of intercourse, as has been discovered by authors of modern sex manuals that show a wide range of possibilities. What is involved here is not simply what couples do with each other but also what they talk about and the extent to which they can acknowledge and recognize each other's sexual needs and fantasies. Those who bring a wide range of experience to their relationship and can share it with their spouse, including some of their fantasy world, are most likely to maintain an active sexual relationship.

One of the reasons Neil's marriage worked well sexually was that he and his wife tried out new things. They "played" with sex. Joe and Mickey, married for twenty years, also found that this worked for them. Joe is a worldly, attractive man who travels widely, flirts easily, and is clearly interested in women and sex. He reads the sex magazines of the different countries he visits, a kind of Cook's tour of the erotic styles of the world. He skirts the edges of respectability by hanging around nightclubs and prostitutes' districts, with a voyeuristic air. He tells Mickey about these. Occasionally she goes with him, especially if they are abroad. He gives her erotic books to read, and they watch films, such as 9½ *Weeks*, together. These experiences stimulate them and give them ideas. They play new roles in bed and occasionally try some of the things they have seen or read about. "I am his sexual ideal. He tells me that my body is exactly what he wants. If I play different roles, he and I are always interested. He doesn't have to do anything elsewhere, though he can look," Mickey says.

Despite the problem of the "Coolidge Effect," which could well lead people into affairs, we want to believe that sex with the same person could always be endlessly fascinating. Admittedly, sex within marriage can be a lot better than sex within briefer, less comfortable relationships. That is the point Ursula makes about her affair with Sean. He may not be much of a lover, but he makes her more excited because she is an "adulterer." This makes her feel sexy and wicked so that within her marriage, where she is comfortable enough to be uninhibited, she has better sex with her husband.

We maintain that sex is largely learned, and mostly within long-term relationships. As Alice said, at the very least couples learn how to help each other to orgasm. But such relationships are also important for another, perhaps more basic kind of sexual learning: for men, how to bring love and sex together; for women, how to feel comfortable enough to experience eroticism separately from love.

Our sexuality is not simply a biological given. It is a complex part of our social being. Each of us creates it within the social world in which we grow up. Our biology, while part of the process, does not determine what we become or what we do. Our sexual lives are very varied and different: we vary in what we do, who we do it with, how we do it, how often we do it, what we feel about it, and what gives us pleasure. This is determined by the social worlds we live in and our social experiences.

We live within a culture, and each culture has characteristic patterns that permeate all aspects of sexuality. For instance, while female breasts are the focus of men's desire in much of Europe and North America, in other cultures they are of much less interest. In Latin America, buttocks are the focus, rather than breasts. In some societies a homosexual relationship may be an expected phase for young men before marriage, while elsewhere homosexuality is highly stigmatized. Cultures are similarly varied as to whether young women should be virgins when they get married. And they vary as to how women should regard their sexuality—as something passive that will be aroused by the love of a good man, as a source of pleasure for themselves and their partners that they can control, or as something they can use to obtain and maintain a relationship with a man. Attempts to explain this large variety of human action and experience in terms of biology or physiology have been dismal failures. Instead we need to understand sexuality and how it develops in terms of an individual's social development. We learn to become sexual, first indirectly as children, then more particularly in adolescence, and finally in adulthood through our sexual relationships.

Sex and Marriage

Marriage may well be the place in which sex is most natural and comfortable. Couples may have periods of sustained, good and satisfying sex in marriage. Many couples who enter marriage have had wildly wonderful sex, but they do not continue to have that kind of sex all the way through marriage. There may be periods, however, in which they feel as turned on and crazy about each other in bed as they did in the beginning. The point about sex within marriage is that it is widely variable over the days, months, and years.

One thing we do know about is the frequency of sex: it almost inevitably declines over the long run. Studies of the sexual behavior of married couples show that the frequency of sexual intercourse is highest at the beginning of the sexual relationship and declines thereafter. One study indicated that almost half of all U.S. couples were having sex at least three times a week in the first two years of marriage but that less than a fifth of couples married for ten years reached that frequency.

Frequency of sexual intercourse for married couples

Years together	% having intercourse less than once a week	% having intercourse three times a week or more
0-2	17	45
2-10	27	27
10+	37	18

Source: Blumstein and Schwartz, *American Couples* (1983)

Of course figures such as these are an imperfect way of representing a very wide variation in behavior. Patterns vary enormously from couple to couple, and each couple changes over time. Sex usually declines in frequency when there are very young children. Second honeymoons are not uncommon when a couple reaches the point where they start to emerge from the interrupted nights and the constant demands of daily life imposed by young children—a

period when sex may have become the "last chore of the day," as
one woman put it. While frequency of sex may not return to the
level of their first months together, it may be a great deal more frequent than it was when they were absorbed in the activities of their
children. But thereafter a slow decline often sets in again.

Many reasons combine to create a decline in a couple's sex life.
Either or both may feel bored or too tired to bother. Exhaustion and
preoccupation get in the way. Anger and resentment, "the normal
stuff of married life," kill desire, as Alice points out below.
Intercourse is likely to have a different meaning for husbands and
wives. There is evidence to suggest that, at least after the initial
phases of a relationship, women may come to value intercourse
more than men. The reason may not be that they have an increased
desire for sex itself but that making love may provide an opportunity for emotional closeness and sharing with their partner. We
believe men more easily cut off sex from love; for them it frequently
is an experience of erotic release rather than emotional closeness.
This difference in the meaning of intercourse within marriage may
contribute to the decline in frequency for couples.

"It makes me feel even angrier with him when we have sex that
feels mechanical than if we don't have it at all," Alice said. "If I'm
already angry at him—and I often feel angry because of this and
that, and resentments pile up, you know, the normal stuff in married life—I can't bear to have sex with him that just confirms our
alienation from each other. Then, of course, we don't have sex, and
then we get more distant. . . . I don't know what the solution is."

Of course it takes two to tango. Declining frequency may be the
result of the changing behavior of one or both partners. Declining
sexual interest in a habitual partner also seems to play a major role
in the falloff in frequency of intercourse in marriage. As it is put in
Madame Bovary:

> *The charms of novelty, gradually slipping away like a garment,
> laid bare the eternal monotony of passion, whose forms and
> phrases are forever the same.*

What is significant here and of obvious interest for any consideration of extramarital relationships is that the decline is not usually a

falling interest in sex itself but a lack of interest in sex with a particular partner, or the "Coolidge Effect."

There is, however, not just a decline in frequency of sex in marriage over time but also in satisfaction. This mirrors the decline in overall satisfaction, which reaches its lowest level during the childbearing years. If couples stay together, satisfaction tends to improve after the children leave home.

The decline in satisfaction and the drop in sexual activity that goes with it, which are characteristic of Western marriages, may not be a universal phenomenon, however. It has been suggested that Western marriages begin hot and become cooler, while the reverse happens in arranged marriages. It has been said that these couples grow to love one another. No systematic research on marital sexuality exists for arranged marriages—which is perhaps itself a comment on different attitudes toward sexuality—but there are some studies on marital satisfaction. In societies in which arranged marriages are common, similar patterns are found in both love and arranged matches—marital satisfaction seems to decline over the years. Regardless of how a couple feels about each other in the beginning, something about the experience of marriage seems to foster a decline in satisfaction with it.

We suggest that some of the difficulty lies in the difference between men and women in their sexuality. They learn about sex differently, and so it comes to have different meanings for them. How does this happen?

Learning to Be Sexual

1. Childhood and Sexual Development

Since Freud discussed the notion of childhood sexuality it has become conventional to regard children as sexual beings from birth. But this is an adult perspective. It requires one to see all childhood activities that involve genitals, for instance, as sexual in the same way as they would be regarded if adults did similar things. Their meaning for the children may be quite different, however. When parents notice their newborn son's erection, it is quite likely they misunderstand what they are seeing. Babies and children indulge in behavior that we often label sexual, but it may not be sexual at all for the child. "Playing doctor" and undressing and examining each other may be exciting because it is forbidden. But it is not sexual in the same way as adults perceive it. It is important to realize that these games satisfy an understandable curiosity about how bodies are made.

These games also carry other important lessons for children. Through them they come to understand that adults are likely to disapprove of them and may call them "dirty." They learn to play the games in private, hiding them from others, especially adults. They learn guilt and associate it with games involving their genitals. They learn that special rules apply to their genitals: that they should not be talked about or touched in public, that they should be hidden in most situations, and that similar conventions apply to excretion. Excretion and genitals become inextricably linked. Both are to be hidden and are the subject of shame and guilt; both are associated with "dirt." There are class, ethnic, and cultural variations in this, but in general these more or less characterize Western attitudes, which filter down to children.

But gender plays a big role in who learns what. Parents do not treat their daughters and sons the same way. Punishments are greater for girls who touch themselves or talk about "dirty" things in public. And boys are allowed to touch their own genitals—they must do so when they urinate. From a young age boys usually have a number of words that they use for their penis, and adults use these words in conversation with them. Girls do not. As a recent article in a woman's magazine pointed out, even as grown-ups women coyly talk about "down there." There are no comfortable, "politically correct," commonly accepted words for female genitalia.

In childhood, boys and girls learn conventions, attitudes, and rules about the body, genitals, and excretion, and they learn to keep quiet and private about them. Their forbidden nature leads to "play talk" about them with each other—"bathroom humor" in prepubertal boys, in particular. They talk and joke with each other in secret. Indeed, the exchange of information among the peer group before puberty is probably the primary source of knowledge of sexual matters for children. This learning occurs within the context of one gender or the other. Girls learn what girls know, boys learn what boys know, and both learn what is permissible for each. They model themselves on the parent of their own sex. In this way they observe and learn the conventions and rules attached to their own genders. As little men and women in training, they watch how men and women treat each other. In this rather indirect way children learn what they do about sex.

2. Adolescence and Girls

Adolescence marks a change in all this. What children learned about their own and others' bodies gets recast as sexual knowledge. Rules of personal modesty begin to be transformed into rules of sexual conduct. As their adult bodies form, the adolescents' view of themselves changes. So does the world's view of them. Others behave toward adolescents as sexual beings. The knowledge built up during childhood is put together with the new feelings and experiences as adolescents. Having sex or touching bodies becomes part of the boys' and girls' imaginings.

One hallmark of adolescence is the sense of uniqueness. Another is the necessity of keeping some thoughts—particularly about sexual feelings—private, away from parents. Adolescents develop a sense that their discovery of the sexual world is a unique journey being undertaken for the first time, and this further forces their learning of sexuality into the private sphere.

At adolescence the focus for boys and girls begins an even greater divide than in childhood. Girls continue to focus on feelings and friendships, which gets elaborated into an emphasis on intimacy and love. The intense friendships of early childhood, the tears of rejection, and the joys of being chosen as a "best friend" are now brought to bear on the first tentative contacts with boys.

They imagine their relationships with boys as intense and emotional. They talk about these things with their female friends. They discuss the romances they've seen in films and read about in novels; they dissect theirs and others' relationships. They talk about love, in the main, not sex. This is very different from the discussions of boys, which centers much more on sex and less on love.

Feelings that girls have may not be labeled sexual at all. Only with the beginning of kissing and petting, which are understood to be sexual activities, does a girl begin to identify her more diffuse and indefinite feelings as sexual. She may then begin to be aware that she experiences sexual arousal. Orgasm may be experienced first as part of petting—long before intercourse. At this age boys experience orgasm frequently, mostly through masturbation. In contrast, many girls do not experience orgasm until they are in long-term, committed relationships perhaps years later. Women's experience tends to be a long-drawn-out process of learning to be sexual, with arousal increasing with sexual experience.

In Kinsey's research most women reported that they started to masturbate only after they had had intercourse for some time, indicating that as they explored and learned to be sexual, they widened their range of sexual activities. In contrast to men, women tend to have their first orgasm with someone rather than through masturbation (although once they have had one, they may find it easier to have subsequent ones through masturbation than through intercourse, as Shere Hite's research has suggested). Research on women's sexual development suggests that most women developed the capacity to reach orgasm some time after adolescence. In other words, women learned to be sexual and did so at a slower pace than men.

In their early adolescent encounters—in which, research suggests, girls received very little satisfaction—the extent to which girls really wanted sex at all, rather than love, affection, and security, was called into question. Boys were usually the instigators, while girls often went along with it, a price they had to pay for the relationship. And there was still a much higher price for adolescent girls—teenage motherhood, or abortion in the case of unwanted pregnancy, and a risky reputation. Neither of these consequences attached to boys. Girls focused on commitment, with sex often a symbol of it. It did not function as the same metaphor for boys.

3. Adolescent Boys

In contrast most boys have had considerable sexual experience before they enter into any romantic relationship—the experience of masturbation. Through it they learn how to channel and focus their

sexual feelings, with accompanying sexual fantasies. Through masturbation they define what is sexually arousing for them. The
images with which they furnish their masturbatory activities are
taken from the world around them—images that are pornographic
or otherwise clearly erotic, delineating for them what society
defines as an arousing female body. With his head full of erotic
images the adolescent boy begins his first romantic relationship
with a real girl.

Another common, although not universal, experience for boys is
performing mutual masturbation to a pornographic image in
groups. Rather than being a homosexual experience, it is one that
bonds boys as heterosexuals. This experience serves to help boys
develop a shared male heterosexual view of female sexuality, and it
is a performance for the others, a competition of virility. But it is
also an experience of sexual arousal helped by another; the boys
may have to communicate with one another to tell what arouses
and what doesn't. They also might talk about it before and after. In
other words, boys have talked about sex and arousal with another
before they have sex with a girl. Girls have not talked or behaved
like this with anyone, although they may have discussed sex as an
abstraction or as an accompaniment to love.

Since this is how boys come to their first heterosexual experience, the task for them of learning about sex is virtually the opposite of what it is for girls. They have to learn to integrate love,
affection, and emotional closeness with their heretofore solipsistic
sexual experiences. Those experiences call on imagery of completely
objectified women with no desires that contradict their own. No
communication is required. Impelled by cultural values and
imagery about men and sex, which are likely to be strongly reinforced by their now extremely important peer group, their interest
will be in making sexual conquests, achieving intercourse, and getting girls to do what they think girls ought to do (and maybe what
they think girls want, based again mostly on locker room talk rather
than on a relationship with a real live girl).

When a boy does finally have sex with a girl, it is not usually an
especially satisfying experience, although, according to current
research, it is much more likely for the boy to have an orgasm than
the girl. Research shows that most boys' first partners are likely to

be inexperienced. These girls are not likely to be able to make it easy and rewarding. Without a good idea of how to please a girl and without the language or experience for communicating—either verbally or nonverbally—what will please the other person, most young people's initial attempts at intercourse are not very satisfactory.

As we discussed earlier, boys come to define their male identity by separation and by what is not associated with their mothers. In doing so, their skills for achieving closeness, dependency, and emotional expressiveness are not as highly developed as in girls. Yet their girlfriends are looking for closeness, dependency, and emotional expressiveness in their relationships with them; for these girls, sex is an expression of all of these. While for the girls sex may appear to be the price they have to pay for what they're looking for or the currency that accompanies them, for boys it may be quite the opposite. In getting sex they are paying with the currency of closeness.

Eventually boys learn to fuse emotions with sex and girls learn eroticism by way of emotional closeness. In other words, sex is a largely learned activity, learned differently by men and women. It is not surprising, then, that men and women behave differently in matters that pertain to both their emotional and their sexual lives—their marriages and their affairs.

4

The Idea of Modern Marriage

That the man and woman were husband and wife, and the parents of the girl in arms there could be little doubt. No other than such a relationship would have accounted for the atmosphere of stale familiarity which the trio carried along with them like a nimbus as they moved down the road.

Thomas Hardy, *The Mayor of Casterbridge*

HISTORICALLY THERE HAS BEEN A BROAD ASSOCIATION between the rise of the companionate model of marriage—the one we have today—and the increase in divorce, one indicator of the instability of modern marriage. As expectations of what marriage will provide rise, more marriages are bound to fall short. Assuming that the law allows for a way out, some couples will try again with new partners. Remarriage or marriagelike cohabitation have risen hand in hand with divorce: whatever divorce represents, it is clearly not a flight from marriage. Instead it marks a disenchantment with one partner and an attempt to try again with another. The belief in modern marriage remains unshaken.

The growth of the current ideal for marriage of sharing, intimacy, and friendship has been gradual and steady over the last century. Within the decades since World War II it has blossomed markedly. In a survey of marital values in the seventies carried out in Britain, for instance, respondents thought "comradeship and doing things together" were the most important ingredients in a happy marriage, followed by "give and take, consideration, discussing things, and understanding." "Neglect, bad communication, and spouse going out" were thought to be the most common factors wrecking a marriage. Yet comradeship and doing things together were much less important in a survey only twenty years earlier, in the early fifties. But the fact that expectations have risen is closely linked to the growing instability of marriage. The ideal itself contains the seeds of its own destruction. There are conflicts in the model on several fronts, and unless a couple is able to negotiate through them, the marriage will be at risk.

The Modern Ideal: Conflicts and Contradictions

One conflict in our companionate, egalitarian, sharing-together model that a couple has to resolve is whether the marriage is a relationship within which all is shared or each individual is autonomous. This conflict is an old and well-known one, but it has become more acute as the ideal of intimacy between partners has grown. If you love someone, how can you want to spend time with anyone else? Shouldn't couples always go out together? Or indeed, should each need *any* outside friendships at all? Time together is at a premium. As a marriage proceeds, the relationship is expected to change, of course, but it is interesting to note the extent to which spouses often resent changes that dilute the intensity of the early "honeymoon" years.

Here, for example, is Polly, sixteen years into her marriage to Richard (and four years after he has ended an affair):

"We used to do everything together. He always wanted to be home with me. We used to go camping together. We used to go hiking. Sex was great. Why can't we get that feeling back—that desire to be together?" Polly said all this sniffling, fighting back tears as she surveyed the broken hopes of her marriage.

One of the most common events to disturb the intensity of this early phase of a relationship in marriage is the arrival of children. In fact, as Polly went on, she made it clear that it wasn't the affair that changed all their togetherness but the arrival of two demanding children, scarcely eighteen months apart.

In their first marital therapy session, this couple was asked when things did change. Polly answered immediately: "Oh, when the babies came. Definitely. He wasn't around at all. Worked all hours. I was left alone with them. They didn't even *know* him. And I was just exhausted all the time." These words came through coated with bitterness.

Indeed, research has consistently shown that husbands and, especially, wives report a sharp decline in their marital satisfaction when children arrive on the scene. Although children remain very much a part of the ideology of marriage, they do make it very hard for a couple to have that all-important time for each other. Children also conflict with the marital ideal in another way. The ideal of shared, common activities is relatively easy to sustain when there are no children. Both members of a couple may be working, but leisure time can be spent together.

And the egalitarian part of the ideal can be easily expressed in how the domestic chores are divided. Washing dishes, cooking, shopping, laundry—these can usually be shared equally. But that all changes when children arrive. That is the point when women do more—the home and hearth become hers, and the husband "helps." Equality goes out the window. Someone has to be in charge of the children, overseeing their welfare in all its mundanity. Nine times out of ten it is the mother. Household demands increase, and she is the one who at the very least oversees them and assigns them—that is, if she does not assume most of them herself. Indeed, many women either give up work when their children are small or take part-time employment. Certainly, in comparison to their husbands, even if working full-time, women spend less time at work than men. The net result of this is that even unwittingly the husband's career takes priority over the wife's. This does not sit well with the ideal of equality.

"Steven's off again this week—to Birmingham or Atlanta or wherever, maybe Detroit," said Marie, the mother of two small children and stepmother (living with her half-time) of an older one. She is a veterinarian, and her husband is a consultant. He is a high-flier, something she used to be. Since they began their family (her stepchild came to live with them part-time after their younger child was born), she has taken a part-time research job so that she can spend more time with her family. Formerly a high flier herself, she no longer is invited to conferences and has moved to the margins of her profession.

Recently, feeling decidedly unsexy after the birth of two children, undynamic after sacrificing much of her career, and neglected by her often absent husband, Marie had a short fling with a coworker, ending it when it looked as if her husband might find out. It shocked her—the prospect of destroying her marriage. Resentment of her husband has not completely subsided, but she has settled into her life with somewhat more measured acceptance these days. "I just don't listen to where he's going. Then I don't get jealous," Marie said. But envy of her husband remains. As does a sense of loss of promise both in her career and in her marriage.

Indeed, one could suggest that wives are double losers in the autonomy stakes. Not only are they responsible for the housekeeping and child care but their traditional role as emotional housekeepers means they are more submerged in the marital relationship. While the husband retains and often increases his status in the world of work and in his life outside the home and the marriage, his wife—especially if she leaves work or changes to part-time work while rearing children—is likely to lose some, if not all, of the autonomy and social contacts that work brings, as well as the intimacy of the love relationship, which children shatter.

Another conflict concerns sex inside and outside marriage. Over the last century we have become a more sexually active society. While this has been a gradual change, it has become more marked since World War II and particularly with the generation that came of age in the 1960s. It might be concluded from this that attitudes toward extramarital sex have become more tolerant. In fact the reverse is true.

Until recently ideas of marriage have been marked by a double standard. In theory monogamy ruled, but in practice there was an expectation that men would stray. Advice books well into the pre-

sent century were clear on the point. Women should hope for a
faithful husband but should not become too upset if he fell short of
the ideal. But of course, the same latitude was not granted to
women. If they behaved like men, they could expect their marriage
to end. Even in the 1950s the advice offerd in women's magazines
still reflected these attitudes. One columnist told a fifty-year-old
woman who discovered her husband had been having a long affair
that "men of this age feel a compulsion to have a fling before age
finally engulfs them." The affair, she assured the suffering wife,
would "die a natural death." Another wife whose husband was in
love with his secretary was advised as follows: "I think your husband
is under the spell of an infatuation that will pass in time and *all you
can do* is wait patiently until it does." (Italics ours.)

By the 1970s women were being given quite different advice.
Erring husbands should not be forgiven; they should be pitied for
doing something so wrong. They needed understanding. *Why* would
a husband start another relationship? What is *wrong* with yours?
Rebuild your relationship through increased understanding, women
were commanded. Intimacy and communication, the relationship
bywords, were stressed, and infidelity was not to be forgiven or
passed over.

Opinion surveys conducted during the 1960s and up to the
1980s also show a strengthening of belief in monogamy. Such a
trend may seem surprising in light of the general liberalization of
attitudes toward sex, but attitudes toward sex inside and outside
marriage are clearly very different. Once *marriage* comes into the
picture, the picture itself changes. Indeed, it is the very rise in sexual relationships outside marriage—especially before it—that has
increased the emphasis on monogamy in marriage; for it is
monogamy that makes marriage different from the other sexual
relationships that have preceded it.

And open marriage, touted in the late sixties and early seventies
as the coming thing, has not come to pass. Researchers seeking
open-marriage couples for studies have usually had to be content
with a handful of respondents.

Pushing in the other direction, from the religious right, have
been increasingly loud voices calling for a return to "traditional"
values, to halcyon days when there were no affairs and less sex

before marriage. In fact, though, marriages have always encompassed affairs; they existed in Victorian (or "traditional") times. But what has changed are the kinds of affairs people have and with whom they have them, as well as the number of affairs.

Sam, for instance, did not take the view that his affairs were right. "I *wish* that I could have the kind of marriage in which I did not have affairs," he said. He was sad, really sad, when he said this. He pined for a relationship that would "give [him] everything." He wished he loved his wife as much as she loved him, because a marriage *should* be faithful, he fervently believed.

Where does this increased emphasis on fidelity—at least in theory if not in practice—come from? As we have hinted already, we think the changed view of marriage actually leads to the greater emphasis on fidelity. As love and sharing become the central themes of marriage, exclusivity becomes expected. If a marriage provides everything, what is the attraction of another relationship? Indeed, any other relationship becomes a threat.

Pat, an extremely beautiful fifty-six-year-old woman, had a stable but not very happy marriage for thirty-three years. She describes her husband as follows:

"He is always so worried about me. If I go out, he wants me to call when I get there. If I'm driving someplace new, he frets about the car. He *seems* to be concerned about my welfare, but I know better. He wants me to be completely dependent on him because he doesn't trust me on my own. He's jealous of every other man I talk to, looking for possibilities everywhere. Which is a little problematic since I work with other men, I have to talk to my doctor who's a man, and so on. . . ."

She looks exhausted by it all as she recounts her long struggle to cope with her husband's marital insecurity.

The commitment to marriage is expressed in love, the shared social life and leisure time, and the promise of sexual exclusiveness. Part of this new focus on the sexual exclusivity of marriage comes from the need to demonstrate its special quality in a world in which sexual relationships among the unmarried are commonplace. With the development of companionate marriage has come the rise in the importance of the wedding. Weddings have become the public notice of the uniquely committed relationship.

Even though Bobbie and Dave had lived together for four years and Dave had been married before, their wedding took place over four days, cost in the tens of thousands of dollars, and of course featured a pristine white wedding dress, the former symbol of chastity. Bobbie's father gave her away. Dave's mother cried as if she were losing him for the first time. A bouquet was thrown and caught by one of the giggling bridesmaids, who was herself living with her boyfriend.

This is in sharp contrast to the wedding in the early seventies of Dave's sister, who also had been living with her boyfriend. At that time the couple's living together, which caused the parents no little embarrassment, was felt to make a mockery of the traditional wedding ceremony. Although there was a large public celebration, Dave's sister felt she could not in good conscience wear a traditional white dress; she substituted a shorter cream-colored one, without a veil. Wedding vows were written, quoting poets who stressed intimacy as well as lust (the "Song of Songs" was read). Everyone stood around in a circle so that the father did not "give his daughter away."

That type of ceremony has become more traditional since then. The rising rates of the number of couples living together without marriage have done little to diminish the importance of weddings; rather, the reverse is true. Because couples cohabit, the wedding marks the start of something *really* different. Most couples not only marry now but have a "real" wedding, not the toned-down type that Dave's sister had.

Even in our secular society, about half of the weddings take place in a church or synagogue. For a significant number of people their wedding is the only religious service they have ever attended. But even when a marriage is not part of a religious ceremony, it is usually a very important social occasion. Spending on wedding receptions has increased, and a growing industry provides the necessary goods and services. Dave and Bobbie not only had flower arrangers and caterers, but they also had a disc jockey, video and still photographers, and a separate wedding cake consultant. Weddings must be seen to be done. In addition, weddings must be reviewed after they are over. This was neatly illustrated by a recent account in a local paper of a couple whose wedding video was ruined by a faulty camera. They took the practical solution and invited everyone back a week later to film it all over again.

Very rare today are brides who are virgins, but the white wedding dress is not a thing of the past. Indeed, the new emphasis on the symbolic and public aspects of weddings may be understood as an assertion that this relationship is different from all other relationships the bride and groom have had in the past. It is entered into with a *symbolic* virginity. At weddings where past lovers of both spouses are part of the crowd that waves the couple off on their honeymoon, the symbolism of the white dress, the veil, the cutting of the cake, and the throwing of the bouquet takes on a different meaning. Marriage is set off as a unique experience. Monogamy within it, a kind of virginity within marriage, is what is now entered in when you exchange vows.

There are many reasons why people are having more affairs now. The built-in conflicts of the marital ideal and disappointment resulting from unrealistically high expectations are chief among these. But there are other reasons. Close loving relationships between the unmarried are now often sexual. Close loving relationships can easily become sexual after marriage as well. This is the final built-in conflict within contemporary marriage. While Victorian husbands (but not wives) would find their extramarital partners outside their own social class (among servants, employees, and prostitutes), today's affair partners are likely to be husbands and wives within the couple's own social class—people with whom they have become close and loving. Affairs of this kind can be more threatening to a marriage—because they can become one.

How Did We Get Here? The Evolution of the Modern Ideal

Industrialization changed not only the economic face of the world but its social one as well. Part of this social change can be seen in the motivations for marriage. The origins of our companionate ideal can be traced back to the burgeoning Victorian middle class. This was a time of intense status-consciousness: where you lived, how many servants you had, and to whom you were married marked how important you were in society. This was a shift away from having status locked ineluctably into who one's family was. As readers of novels from that time are aware, a good marriage to someone of wealth and position was crucial for a man's career, while for a woman it was almost her only chance to move away from her parental home. Love at this point was not the central motivation for marriage—securing appropriate social position was. Love was not entirely irrelevant, but it was certainly not enough. If the two families being joined by marriage objected to the match, it did not take place. The absence of love was no bar to a marriage's occurrence.

As for sex, a man was expected to enter marriage having had sexual relationships. His wife certainly was not. His liaisons would have been with a prostitute, a paid mistress, or a servant. All of them would likely have been from a lower social class than his. Whatever else may be said about the Victorian era, its marriage procedures were not particularly likely to lead to satisfactory sexual relationships. Equality of sexual enjoyment was not a notion yet on the horizon. The sexual relationships the man had were not models or learning experiences for marriage.

Clearly, sex as means of communication of love or something to be equally enjoyed by husband and wife were often foreign notions during this time. Instead, men's past sexual relationships were likely to become a source of guilt and anxiety. Since middle-class Victorian wives were assumed not to have sexual desires, they became easy repositories for the guilt and anxiety their husbands felt. Talk about sex between husbands and wives would have been difficult, and a well-brought-up woman would have considered it offensive.

There was little chance, therefore, for sex to become a happy and satisfying part of the marital relationship. Sometimes all went well, but this was despite the prevailing notions and habits. This setup encouraged men to continue their pursuit of sex outside marriage—again, among lower-class women.

The economic uncertainties of life among the less prosperous classes made permanent marriage less likely. There was not always expectation of marriage at all. But as government power extended, marriage was encouraged. States wanted to have marriages registered. This drew a much stronger line between the married and the unmarried. The beginnings of health and welfare provisions also encouraged these trends. Pensions, housing, and subsidized medical care became available—but only to families of workers. This encouraged marriage and family life. Gradually as more people married they began to aspire to marriages that looked like those of the upper classes.

But in these marriages men's and women's worlds were very separate. The social lives of men were with men, and women's were with women. Women organized the home and supervised the servants, and men went out to the world of work. Again as readers of Victorian novels will know, after dinner men went into the library to smoke their cigars and drink their port, while women retired first to the powder room and then to the drawing room to gossip—without the men. Indeed, in certain bastions of old-world tradition, such practices persist today. (The Garrick Club, a private London club whose membership is drawn particularly from people in the theater, journalism, and the law, recently voted not to admit women. "Women are just not clubbable" was one member's explanation. As guests of these highly clubbable men, women are now allowed in the corridors of the Garrick—but only certain corridors. The rest are closed to them.)

There were critics of this form of marriage even before the turn of the century. Experiments in alternative forms had already been tried. The Oneida Community, in which marriage and family life were communal, was set up in 1847. At its height it had over two hundred men, women, and children. Some marriage manuals of this time were beginning to mention how marriage might demean women and how it did not take their sexual feelings into account. Mutual respect and friendship were beginning to become the central ideal of marriage. World War I accelerated these trends. This war provided a range of employment for women and made paid employment socially acceptable for them in all social classes. Women had more economic independence, and the disruptions of the war served to widen social horizons. These changes inevitably influenced attitudes toward relationships and marriage. Not far behind the increased independence and freedom for women was more equality in relationships and in marriage. These experiences, together with separations caused by the war, led to a peak in the number of divorces at the end of it. For many who lived through the war it seemed a crucial turning point.

But with the return to peace and of men reclaiming their jobs and power at home came a reassertion of traditional values about women, which meant that there was a push for them to stay at home and accept a lesser role in the marital relationship. Opposition to birth control remained widespread.

The postwar home to which women returned was very different from the one of even a few decades earlier. Economic changes in the labor market led to a large decline in the availability of servants; some of the wealthy had to make do with a cleaning woman who would not live in. Labor-saving devices such as washing machines and vacuum cleaners meant that wives could do much of the domestic work themselves. This included child care. In this way the emphasis was on the home and the family as separately functioning, self-reliant units. The married couple, responsible for running the home in a new way by themselves, had to talk more with each other, even negotiate more, now that they ran it together.

Further developments such as automobiles and the movies meant that there were more leisure-time pursuits for husbands and wives to share. This presented a marked change from married life of even a few decades before.

By this time women were asserting some control over their sexuality as well. During the age of the flapper, legs were shown, hair was cropped, and cigarettes were smoked. Women danced in a more abandoned way and drank more openly. Sexuality was acknowledged: films showed passion, and film stars such as Gloria Swanson could display both dignity and sexuality at the same time. Margaret Sanger began her campaign for contraception, and gradually couples—mainly educated ones—increasingly used it. Ignorance and lack of knowledge became bogeymen—obstacles to a successful sexual relationship—and largely clinical marriage manuals became essentials for couples beginning marriage. These persisted in portraying women as largely passive but did recognize women's needs for sexual satisfaction.

The double standard still existed; this meant it was believed that men were less able to control their sexual urges and so were more likely to have affairs. But at this point they did not pursue such relationships only in the lower classes but increasingly turned to women from their own social groups. In *Tender Is the Night*, Nicole, a wealthy young woman (whose character is based on Fitzgerald's wife, Zelda), has an affair with a friend of her husband's. (Indeed, it sends her to the brink of madness, but in any case, she is not cast out of the social fold for having one.) Eroticism was now possible within marriage, and with women of all classes.

In the inter-war period, women were demanding more from their marital partners, both in and out of bed. The same values—of being "friends," of sharing interests and desires—came to be expected now in relationships between men and women outside of marriage as well. Films and novels of the period stress love as well as desire on both men's and women's parts. Even affairs are now seen to be companionate. Noel Coward's *Brief Encounter* (in which there is an unconsummated affair) shows a man and woman meeting and becoming increasingly intimate and familiar with each other, driven not only by passion but also by shared perceptions and interests. *Brief Encounter* illustrates the fundamental threat of the companionate affair—the modern affair, which, unlike its Victorian predecessor, can all too easily become a companionate marriage.

Just as World War I did before it, World War II had a profound and lasting effect on marriage. Men were gone for years at a time from families they had only just started, and women went to work, often alongside other men. These trends were now coupled with women's ease in both mobility and in social and sexual lives. A generation of women was created who not only had more independence and belief in themselves but also more often had had sexual experience (up to and often including intercourse).

According to Kinsey's research, carried out just after the end of World War II, close to three-quarters of men and about a third of women were not virgins at the time they married. Sexual attitudes and practices had indeed changed. Marriage was a much more erotic proposition. In the fifties, problems about sex began to appear in advice columns of women's magazines. Those seeking advice were told that sex was "an important part of marriage." When one woman wrote complaining that the intimate side of marriage does not appeal to her, she was sharply told, "Your husband has a legitimate grievance. However good you are in other ways, you are failing in part of your duty toward him." Sex and marriage were now inextricably linked. Women who wanted to explore their sexuality had to do it within the confines of marriage. This intensified the bonds between marriage, sex, love, and friendship. Marriage was the place where one "got it all."

During the postwar decades, although women left work to stay home and raise children, their daughters carried the torch they had left behind during the war. These daughters had more education than their mothers, more affluence, and more leisure time; they were able to travel and live away from home (at college, for instance, or at summer camp), and had increased employment prospects and expectations. The generation that came of age in the sixties was one in which the kind of relationship they expected between men and women was that of their mothers and fathers taken one step further: not only would they be friends and partners with their husbands, sharing intimacies in and out of bed, but they would also be equals. This meant not only economic and social equality but also a growing ideal of sexual equality.

From this discussion it should be clear that the increase in permissive sexuality in the sixties was not a sudden occurrence but the result of a gradual recognition that sexual desire was part of everyone's makeup: men and women, both rich and poor. During that time sex was talked about more, and women's sexuality became more open and was increasingly accepted. The wilder shores of sexuality were now in common parlance. In that sense sex was out of the closet. Sex before marriage and cohabitation became institutions. This does not fit well, however, with the unchanged ideal that men and women in a marriage are equals and partners and are lovers and sexual adventurers together. The conflict between sex within marriage and outside of it can be seen to generate specifically from this time. Why should it be stopped by marriage? Men and women are close, confiding, and sexual in marriage, but they can also be so outside of it.

Living Marriage Today

In America one in two marriages now ends in divorce. Increasingly, there may be affairs. The idea of marriage as we know it, like Topsy, "just growed and growed." The inherent instability of marriage, though, makes sober consideration of its inherent conflicts, its inner contradiction imperative.

Kelley and Scott fell in love the first week of college, at the first party each attended. They became inseparable and were married as soon as they graduated. Kelley had had a boyfriend in high school, and she was not a virgin when she and Scott first slept together. Scott had gone to an all boys' Catholic school, and not only was he a virgin, but he also considered Kelley's past a bit sordid. He tried not to think about it, but if they had had a bad day together, he sometimes found himself, when he was tired, morosely dwelling on the fact that he had not been her first. Maybe he wasn't as important to her as she was to him. As for Kelley, she knew her "past" made Scott uncomfortable, but apart from that and little niggling signs of possessiveness on his part, she was very happy. Scott had everything she wanted: he was handsome, smart, liked the same things she liked, and they had similar friends—although not too many, since they liked to stay home and watch T.V. or study or eat or listen to music together. In the summertime they swam and had picnics. They really didn't do much with others because they didn't need to.

When they left college Scott went on to get a law degree at a prestigious university. Kelley took a trainee job at a bank to support them. Scott returned late from classes and the library and was tired on weekends. Kelley cooked, washed, and cleaned. She became friendly with people from her job downtown. She joined a health club and exercised with coworkers after work. Scott was often not home for dinner anyway. She began to stay downtown, going out to eat and sometimes to the movies with some of her new friends. Scott and Kelley began to argue and to get on each other's nerves when they did spend a few hours together during the week. Scott didn't like her new friends and mocked her new obsession with working out at the health club. She was often in tears. And then sex went. After things had broken down badly, Scott phoned for a marital therapy appointment.

At the point this couple started marital therapy, Kelley was so deeply resentful of Scott she could barely talk to him. When she did speak it was to accuse him: "You never do anything. You're only interested in me for sex anyway. We used to do everything together. Now all you want me for is to be your maid and sex slave." It seemed as if they both wanted the same thing—to go back to the way it had been when they were both students, when their schedules and interests were so similar that they could live as if one.

Since Scott could offer Kelley only part of what she wanted—he was not interested in reducing his study time by much, it turned out—she was not interested in negotiating with him. "That's not what I got married for." She spent less time, rather than more, with him. A weekend away was arranged, to give them more time together and to reduce hostilities, but Kelley disappeared. When Scott arrived home that night, he found she had cleared her things from their house, left him a note, and asked that he not try to reach her. Scott later realized that she probably had already begun a relationship with someone else, someone with whom she worked, someone with whom she could become inseparable, who would "love" her in the old, romantic, "marriage-is-for-everything" way.

Contrast this with Laura, a thirty-nine-year-old art restorer who married at twenty-one, had three children, and developed her career after her children were well settled in school. As a schoolgirl she had idolized her husband, a scientist. He seemed to have it all: looks, brains, athletic ability, and popularity. She was thrilled to be going out with him and continued her hero worship well into their early married life. But with the arrival of children, things changed. Laura was a good mother and had a close and warm relationship with her kids. Moreover, she found a group of other mothers from the neighborhood and the school who thought she was funny, charming, and an admirable person in her own right. She came into her own during those years and slowly realized how little her husband appreciated her. True, he thought she was pretty and sweet, a good mother and housekeeper, but he didn't talk to her the way these new and interesting friends did.

After Laura began working, her friendships increasingly included men. Some of these men talked to her the way her women friends did. It wasn't long before affairs with some followed. Laura never stopped respecting her husband, who continued to be a good provider, a sensible and loyal, if distant, husband and father, and a decent, reliable, and good man. Laura had made a clear assessment of her marriage by the time she began to have affairs. Over the years her own requirements for "everything" in the marriage realm had changed. She needed more now than she had needed in the early years, but she concluded that her husband was not the one to fulfill these new needs. He was good at other things. Intimacy was not their strong suit together. Others could step in to fill the breech.

This is one way of resolving the tensions—change your expectations of marriage. But when Annie, whom we met in the first chapter, tried to do this and her husband found out about her last affair, it caused their separation. While having an affair may be an attempt to solve the conflicts posed by living, breathing marriages, it is a risky solution.

5

His Affair/Her Affair

I have never met a woman who experiences sexuality in this depth within a marriage of ten years or more, no matter how much passion she may feel for her husband, no matter with what empathy and precision they have come to know each other's physical needs. It was simply a different order of experience. . . . I have no idea how to integrate this insight with the demand for loyalty, the need for abiding relationships that must often be based on exclusivity when sexuality is involved, the destructiveness of lying to a person whom you love and live with and to whom you are unalterably committed in friendship; and yet the equally intense destruction of allowing him to live with the knowledge that you are involved passionately with someone else.

Jane Lazarre, *On Loving Men* (1981)

*I*t SHOULD BE CLEAR BY NOW THAT IN ORDER TO UNDERSTAND the varied phenomena we call affairs we first need to refer to marriage and how people are managing to live within it. While our society may not have a clear definition of what an affair means, we do have a well-defined view of the ideal marriage. It is companionate and romantic. It stresses intimacy and togetherness. While there is a nod toward the needs of the individual, the criteria for intimacy of the couple are much better spelled out than those for autonomy. That means there is much room for individual judgment and maneuvering when determining the boundaries between the marriage and the individual. This maneuvering includes sexual conduct. Sometimes marriages have an articulated code of sexual marital conduct, but more often, apart from the original marriage vows that call for monogamy, they do not. Sometimes what happens is that over time the two individuals in the marriage evolve their own codes of conduct. These may change as the marriage changes, without discussion between the spouses. These codes may remain individual and private.

Undisclosed and undiscovered, an affair can remain a private matter. In theory, it may never challenge a marriage. But once an affair becomes known, the private, individual understanding of what is permissible within marriage becomes the shared domain of both spouses. It poses clear questions and choices about the boundaries between autonomy and sharing for that marriage. How marriage is defined by the partners is obviously a central component in dissecting affairs. What is the experience of an affair and how does it relate to marriage?

In novels, in research, and in personal accounts of affairs we often encounter attempts to classify what is being related and what has happened. We need this because we are confronting something shocking. Affairs fly in the face of stated convention, if not statistically common practice. What sort of affair are we hearing about or having? Is it a one-night stand, a serious love, an ongoing sexual alliance? Does it threaten the marriage? Has it been going on for a long time? How often do the lovers meet? How much of their time does it occupy? Is it secret? If anyone knows, who is it? Is the affair in retaliation for a past affair? Would or does the spouse mind?

Each of these questions represents an attempt to classify some dimension of the situation and suggests that the answer will determine how we should think about the affair and react to it. However, underneath these attempts to manage or understand affairs are some very basic assumptions that do not get articulated. We think they can be the most important ones. We may not even realize that these largely unarticulated assumptions govern our marriages and help to explain the why, the how, and indeed the *why not* of any affair. In addition, they may help to account for the different impacts affairs have on marriages. These assumptions about marriage and its functions are thus about the relationship between affairs and marriage. These run deep in our thinking. They underlie all work, both clinical and research, on affairs as well as the attempts made by people in affairs to understand their individual experiences. We think in order to understand the phenomenon of affairs and marriage it is vital to unearth these basic assumptions that exist within the framework of present-day companionate marriage.

Although attempts have been made to classify affairs, there have been fewer attempts to classify the models or views or expectations of marriage that give rise to affairs. Nevertheless, much of what has been written or reported about affairs and marriage explicitly or implicitly takes one of the following views:

1. *The affair is a symptom of something wrong with the marriage.* This view holds that an affair is essentially indicative: if the marriage were good, then there would be no need for the affair. Often the meaning of the affair is taken to indicate exactly what was wrong with the marriage. For example, if the affair is sexually satisfying, this points to a sexual weakness in the marriage. Annie's affair when her first child was eight months old is a case in point. She wondered whether or not she would ever be considered sexy again.

In addition to the experience many women report of finding motherhood incompatible with sexiness, Annie also had another problem. From the beginning of her marriage, she had been unsure whether her husband really desired her. She reports that he married her under pressure and was ambivalent about her at the time, when she thought—wrongly—that she was pregnant. Although their sexual relationship was technically satisfying, Annie was inhibited by her insecurity about her desirability. When sex dwindled after the birth of their first child, she thought it might have dwindled permanently and that it reflected an underlying truth of their sexual relationship. Her first affair, which was intensely erotic—Annie claims to have had no illusions about its emotional depth—served to affirm that she was sexy, at least to someone. Most of all she could feel unabashedly sexy about herself. The other question remained—did her husband desire her? The affair did not address that one, at least not directly, but it did lend Annie a welcome aura of sexiness.

Similarly, this view would hold that if the affair was deeply intimate; it would indicate that the marriage was not intimate enough. Or if the affair was exciting, this would point to the need for the marriage to become more exciting. Most clinical work, such as marital therapy, begins with this assumption. (In chapter 7 we will look a bit further at some of the issues raised in therapy with marriages in which there has been an affair.)

2. *The affair is an enhancer to a satisfactory marriage and can make it even better; an affair does not necessarily harm marriage.* This view is usually espoused by proponents of open marriage and is often accompanied by more or less explicit contracts. Spouses are permitted to have extramarital relationships because such relationships are assumed to be enhancing. It is assumed that what is enhancing for one partner will improve the whole marriage.

Ursula said that David's affairs made her happy because he was happy when falling in love. David was pleased that Ursula found out she could do something forbidden; it unleashed her carnality with him. This position is often stated in a different form: if extramarital relationships were not permitted, this would mean the marriage was entrapping or suffocating, denying the partners' respective personal growth and thus stifling the joint enterprise of marriage since the individuals within it would feel stifled. "I couldn't do that to him," is the way Ursula would say it; "It would just be absurd to stunt her like that," would be David's assessment.

These two views are widely held, sometimes explicitly, but usually implicitly, and are very often evident in people's own reports of their affairs. The first is the view most prevalent in our culture.

3. A third view that we find surfacing in reports people give of their extramarital relationships is that *the affair has little direct relationship with the marriage itself.* In their general assessments of their lives, everything is interrelated for many people. But others do not experience any significant overlap in terms of how they define and demarcate their marital relationships and their affairs, any more than they see their work lives overlapping their marriages or friendships, or their platonic friendships overlapping their marriages. They feel comfortable with the separation between the two and find this separation clarifies their marriage.

As we have seen, Laura is one who segmented her marriage; for her, affairs were part of the reason her marriage worked. She never received an intensity of emotions or deep intimacy from her husband, but she enjoyed his companionship. She received appreciation of some of the qualities in herself that she esteemed (good wife, good mother, pleasant and attractive person), and she and her husband shared a long history, a stable home, and deep devotion to their children. Laura does not mourn what she does not have with him. Instead she prizes what she does have.

Laura said, "That's not him," when talking about men who expressed their feelings. "But he is a very devoted father and a good man." She attached these qualities to marriage and the family. "Great sex" is the way she described a man with whom she had an affair. Great sex was the province of the affair. "That's not what I get with him [her husband], either," she said, but she managed with comfortable, if infrequent, sex and felt warmly about her husband when they made love.

Each of these views depends on an idealized notion of marriage. In the first, marriage should be for everything; any interactions that are romantic, sexual, or overlap with marriage compete for interest, energy, and time with the spouse and so encroach on what is rightfully in the marital domain.

In the second, marriage is seen as being essentially for the growth of the individual and consequently not sexually sacred or exclusive. This is the so-called open marriage. Usually, however, other qualities of marriage are defined as exclusive and are preserved in the implicit or explicit contract. For example, intimacy may be exclusive; no one is allowed to get too close with the partner in the affair. Or place may be special; there are injunctions about where an affair may be carried on—such as "never in our bed/house/town/in front of the neighbors."

Often, but not always, the emphasis in these marriages is on shared honesty, which is held to increase intimacy and confirms it as the central facet of what makes the marital relationship special. "We let each other grow. We are tough enough to accept our spouses having affairs, because our love for the other and consequently our respect for his/her personal growth is so great." These other aspects, not sexual monogamy, define the marriage and what is special about it.

Things are not so clearly laid out in the third view. This is the situation in which at least one of the spouses has begun a process of redefining the functions of his or her marriage. The affair may help to clarify what is in the marital domain. It is a view that accepts a segmentation of marriage. It does not push marriage to be for everything. But unlike in an open marriage, the retreat from the original marital ideal is not explicit. One or both of the partners may privately adopt the segmented marriage model, which acknowledges autonomy more fully than the model in which marriage is for everything. It provides a basis from which to pursue an affair. These affairs remain undisclosed and often remain undiscovered. If the marriage does benefit from an affair of this kind, it is because the segments of the marriage that function best have been clarified.

"My husband cannot give me intimacy or intensity," says Laura. "My affairs do." Laura discovered that it helped her to accept her husband if she sought romance and sexual excitement from other men. Once she accepted that, rather than agonizing over whether she should break up her family to pursue an ideal man, her marriage became markedly more stable. The benefits to which Laura testified may accrue, but they clearly depend on secrecy, an issue central to the conduct and effect of affairs, and one we will discuss further in chapter 7.

Christina began an affair with a colleague when there was a series of changes in her life: her children had both gone off to school, she had recovered from an incapacitating physical condition, and she had begun to commute to the city part-time to reestablish herself in her old career. She began to feel free and alive again. Part of that came from an attractive and sympathetic colleague with whom she eventually began an affair; he knew her in the context of her professional life rather than her former all-embracing one of mother and wife.

She had no desire to impose her new work concerns on her husband since these interests had never drawn them together. Instead, the demarcation between her career and home life, evident in the geographical and temporal separation between the two, also existed in her emotionally. Marriage could be separated from work. Emotions could be separated from marriage. This revised view of her marriage evolved in silence. She did not know whether her husband shared her conclusions, nor did she risk finding out. Secrecy was her chosen strategy.

The double pressure that marriage be for everything and that people be together for a lifetime means that, over time, a large proportion of married people will feel that marriage has let them down in one respect or another. We are not surprised, therefore, that the view that marriage and affairs can be totally separate appears with some frequency in the stories in this book. Dividing a marriage into segments—some of which work and some of which do not—is an understandable response to the real experience of marriage. What is surprising is that while some people come to the realization that if some facets of their lives can be segmented off from their marriages, so can their sexual conduct (even though this goes against the marital covenant), others who also divide their marriages into segments do not.

"I did not feel guilty," Laura reported about her first affair. She looked a bit embarrassed saying it. "I really didn't! I had a wonderful time with that man, and I have a lot of affection for him now. He certainly did not hurt my marriage. If my husband had found out, I would have felt guilty. Looking back I realize I took risks. But at the time I felt no guilt, and even now I don't because he actually helped me to be happier. Can you understand that? I know that sounds funny, but it's true."

Most marriages begin in the marriage-is-for-everything model. They may become segmented later, but not necessarily in sexual matters. In every marriage couples grapple with difficult negotiation points. We are referring to something more than differences in taste and whim. At various points in life something critical occurs for one member of the couple that either runs counter to the other's wishes and values or takes one spouse in a different direction, away from the other. This could be, for instance, a job, a career change, a development of a new but important interest, or an addition to the family through birth or a child's marriage.

It should be obvious that changes *within* the couple and events *outside* the marriage both conspire to effect changes over time. The result often is that one member of the couple spends more time and energy apart from the other. The nature of the intimacy with which the marriage began changes. Intimacy may come to exist in certain areas but not others. The resulting moments of intimacy may be deeply satisfying, but over time in a marriage intimacy is rarely, if ever, all-encompassing.

At each "negotiation point" for the couple there is an increased chance that autonomy will win out over intimacy. If the marriage survives, people adapt to this process by expecting certain rather than all things from their spouses. There is an inevitable shift toward more autonomy as the marriage unfolds, particularly when children arrive.

When Christina and her husband married, they went off to Latin America, where he was working on his doctoral thesis. Christina, not yet altogether sure what she ultimately wanted to do with her life, went along and helped by teaching in the village, learning about the tribal ways, and gathering data for the research. This Latin American interlude in the earliest years of their marriage reflected and intensified the absorption and self-containment this couple had with each other. It was a happy time, but it ended when the couple moved on to the next phase of their life together—jobs, children, and setting up a permanent home. Each of these changes fostered a new distance between them.

Their house was an old one, and to save money the husband did much of the renovation. Since this work also coincided with the birth of their children, Christina spent that much more time with the children. When he returned from work, her husband often worked on the house. They were often tired, but sex, she reported, had always been good. Her husband was passionate about her and always desired her. But then her old dance injuries began to cause problems, exacerbated by carrying small children around, and she was bedridden for a long time. Sex became impossible, so even that intimacy became further truncated. Yet they found a different way of feeling close to each other: a sense that they were creating a home and family that was theirs. When her husband was not working at his job or on the house, the family went on walks, trips, visits, and to events together. They played games in the backyard, played music, and watched videos together. Both of them watched their two children grow, and they delighted in them equally and loved each other for that equal delight in their children. In other words, although they spent less time with each other, talked less to each other, and had sex with each other less often, they loved each other no less. A different kind of connection had grown between them.

Christina had an affair to fill the void of the intimacy, the absorption in each other that they had once had. Others fill the void with other things—friends, work, and so forth—or wait until there is more time for each other again.

"I think of marriage as being like that Stanley Donen movie, *Two for the Road,* only without the bitterness and the moral that marriage is so brittle it's bound to break," said Alice, a writer and mother of two who has been married to an academic for eighteen years. She has not had an affair, nor does she think that her husband has. But she has adjusted her view of her marriage many times over the years and said that "I haven't stopped assessing it yet. It's a bit like coming out of shock—you only know what the effect of a change has been when you're just about out of it. When our first child was born, I thought at first that I had never known what love was *really* like before because not only did I love this tiny person more than anything else ever before, but I loved my husband so very much more because he was part of our son and loved him as I did. I knew how much I did, so I knew how much he did. It was like a big balloon of intense love surrounding us. But then I went into a period of hating him more intensely than ever before partly *because* my connection with our son was more intense than with him.

"The usual had happened: my work took on much less importance—voluntarily, I must say—and so I worked a lot less. His work became slightly less important for about a month, and then it was back to his normal, driven, workaholic routine, which had been one of the great attractions about him for me in the beginning. He was so wonderfully focused and successful. But now I resented it. We fought a lot. Sex felt beside the point for me. Anyway, I was fat. After two years I finally realized this *was* my life; it wasn't going to go back to normal [that is, before babies]. I started to feel more accepting of him again. I began to work more as our son began to go to day care more, and that seemed to be right for him. So I had more time on my hands.

"Then we moved, because my husband got a new job, and my father died and I had a second child—all within the next two years. And it was back to the feelings of estrangement and anger again. I thought I absolutely knew that my marriage was always going to be distant and unfriendly. But our children were getting older and were starting school and nursery school, and we began to find time to go to the theater, movies, and restaurants again—things we had formerly done and enjoyed. I slowly found that my husband was still someone who was funny and wise, and he had actually noticed what was happening to me during all the time we had been stony with each other. So then I had to think differently about him and my marriage again.

"Here we were, about fifteen years down that road, still together, walking together a little more closely and with more enthusiasm again. Not quite as in the beginning—with our bodies intertwined, taking steps together, and not noticing anyone or anything else— but in some ways better. I like having space. I like having time to see friends, to work, and to have the kids on my own. I just don't want that to be all. And I like having him as a friend again, probably the best one I have but certainly not my only one."

Although Alice had considered affairs and had had a deep flirtation with one, as she put it, she has never had one. "Because I'd be too scared," she said. "I wanted to have affairs when things felt lousy between my husband and me. And if I'd had an affair, I might have left him. But for what? Just as I know that marriage keeps changing, I know that the affair, now a marriage, would also. And to what? And my marriage *might* get better—which it did after each low point. I think in the long term like that, which is why I've never had one."

In this naturally evolving fashion every marriage moves away from the marriage-is-for-everything ideal from which it starts. Ideals being ideals and not real, however, this formula still remains the one people continue to espouse, despite their reality. And just because there is increased autonomy in other areas does not mean that there is sexual autonomy. When sex is involved, the stakes and issues shift into a different gear.

If a long-term marriage does not have to fulfill every domain, what are its functions? If people are able to segment their marriages, into what segments do they fall? As we shall see, the answers to these questions begin to suggest some categories of affairs.

Segmenting Marriage: The Four Dimensions of Marriage

It seems reasonable to divide the experience of marriage into four dimensions. These are the public, the practical, the emotional, and the sexual. By these we mean the following:

The *public dimension* refers to the roles the spouses portray in their joint social life, and the ease and enjoyment with which the couple and their family participates in the social world.

Tessa and Craig, for example, are very involved with their children's school and in politics. They are seen, and experience themselves, as a couple who work well and in harmony with each other in the organizational and social functions these two activities demand. "I like Craig. He's very good at parties, at meetings. He's very easy and cooperative. He's very reasonable. We have never had any trouble with scheduling things, helping each other out, that kind of thing. But he's just not someone I can talk to about a lot of things. I don't find him very interesting. He doesn't understand a lot of my points when I talk about books I've read or about people. He's not very interested in what makes people tick, and I am. But he's very easy to live with, on the level of practical details and our social lives running smoothly, and on the importance of commitments to social and political engagements."

The social dimension of a marriage may be a most fulfilling and important one for a couple, or it can be very empty. Or, for another couple, it may not be very important to share an intense and full social life.

Laura, the art restorer, came to expect, especially when her children were small, that most of her social life would be in the company of women and children. As the children grew up and she returned to work, her social life included colleagues from her world of work. Her husband, a solitary man in contrast to Laura's gregariousness, shied away from this world. He participated little in her social life, but she was not troubled by this. Indeed, she relished the freedom his withdrawal brought.

The *practical dimension* encompasses domestic and daily activities that demand the couple's cooperation. For instance, Craig and Tessa comfortably apportion child care, cleaning, cooking, and bill-paying. Unlike many couples, each feels greatly supported by the other in the maintenance of family life. Again, the organizational aspects of a shared domestic life can be supportive or obstructive in a couple's life together. Or it can be a non-issue. Some women may take over domestic organization, for instance, while their husbands assume financial responsibilities, with neither arguments nor resentment.

The *emotional dimension* embraces empathy, friendship, support, shared interests and values; understanding and ease of communication, especially of feelings, values, and deep concerns; and the degree of intellectual rapport and stimulation a couple experiences together. Tessa, for example, said she feels as though she is "talking Greek to Craig when I mention things that interest me. He just doesn't get it. Sometimes he doesn't even understand the words I use."

In contrast, Michael, a middle-aged father of three, said that he says "everything to Jennie [his wife]." She is "my best friend." And Jennie concurs: "There is nothing I keep from him. His perspective is always useful and interesting." They share many, if not all, interests, including gardening, walking, swimming, reading novels, seeing movies, and eating. Indeed, at this point in their lives this couple feels very fortunate to be satisfied not only in this dimension of marriage but also the other three.

This has not always been the case. A few years ago Jennie felt almost abandoned by Michael, left out of his life in favor of his work and diminished by his relative lack of interest in their three children's development. Their marriage demonstrates the point about the evolution of any given marriage. The quality of their relationship has improved in every area as their children have grown and as Michael has become less anxious about his career. There is now both more overlap of interest and more time spent together, and their capacity for a deeper friendship has developed.

The *sexual dimension* refers to the sexual satisfaction, pleasure, excitement, freedom, and interest that a couple experiences together. Tessa, for instance, would rate her happiness in this dimension as low, while rating her happiness in the public and practical dimensions as high. "Since I'm not so interested in Craig as a person, I don't feel strongly attracted to him. I don't feel he really knows me since I don't think he understands me. Our sex life is pretty low-key and not all that exciting. But he's a low-key person, so it doesn't seem to get to him." In contrast, Nicholas and Debbie had an embattled fourteen-year marriage that ended in divorce. Yet for them sex was always fulfilling, interesting, and pleasurable.

Again, there is a wide range in both satisfaction with and the importance of the sexual dimension in marriage. As we saw in chapter 3, the sexual and emotional dimensions are particularly subject to changes and fluctuations in a marriage over time.

One member of a couple may feel more or less happy with each of these dimensions, while the other may not. In addition, the satisfaction and comfort levels with each may fluctuate over the lifetime of the marriage. Craig is reasonably happy with both sex and the level of intimacy in his marriage, while Tessa is not. Yet earlier in the marriage she was happier with sex and was also more tolerant of the gaps in their mutual understanding.

For many, not being content with one aspect of a marriage does not mean they will seek satisfaction in an affair, as Alice has already testified. But for others, discontent is either the motivation for beginning an affair or the glue that ensures its continuation. Yet these people may feel very devoted to their marriages because they are happy in its other dimensions.

Tessa has always received her emotional sustenance primarily from her friends and colleagues. Sex has fluctuated in importance for her, and in any case she and Craig have been at least moderately compatible with each other. Recently she began an affair with a colleague. This was not her first affair, but the others had occurred when she was on business trips, and they were not continued. Thus, she thought, they did not threaten her marriage. The current affair is different because it is open-ended, although her lover definitely does not want her to leave her husband. This is disturbing to Tessa only because it disturbs her pride. She wants to be desired *totally* even though she is unavailable.

Tessa does not want to give up what is in many respects an easy and comfortable marriage. She does not want her children's lives to be disturbed or become unstable because her marriage is unhappy and rocky and might break up. She does not want to give up the circle of friends and the political connections she and Craig have cultivated. "Why should I do that?" she asks. "He doesn't know about it. It doesn't affect him that I'm sleeping with someone else, talking seriously and sympathetically with someone else. It's not on his time. It's not taking anything away from him that he had before or that he would get anyway." Despite her passion for her lover, she remains attached to Craig and deeply sustained by the smooth and supportive public and practical functioning of their marriage.

Segmenting Affairs: The Four Dimensions of Affairs

If marriages can be segmented, so can affairs. While potentially any affair may be important on these same four dimensions, some of the dimensions may not be present in the affair or may not be very salient. Most people, for instance, put boundaries around their affairs to ensure that there is no public dimension at all. This is critical in a secret affair, but even in open marriages, most people try to conduct their affairs with more than a little discretion, hiding them at least partly from the public eye. Clearly, there is a sexual dimension in affairs, but this may not be its most salient characteristic (at least for the people in the affair).

Ursula's affair with Sean illustrates that: "He's not as good a lover as David, but he makes me feel like an adulteress. Then I am sexy. Sexier with David." But "he is someone who understands art in the same way. It's a very poetic relationship. Very romantic." This is the dimension she values most in her affair with him.

Similarly, the emotional dimension of an affair may be more or less important or satisfactory. For Tessa, as she has said, both of these dimensions were extremely important and satisfying. In contrast, Annie's first affair was very sexual but emotionally cool, while David's affair on a business trip was sexually satisfying and emotionally hot during its short duration. This was an affair he had while in California on business. The meetings were intense, the sunshine was heavenly, and the evenings were free. "I fell 'in love' again. Lovely feeling. I told her I was married. It was an intense, wonderful time. It ended. I went back and thought, 'That's that.' I was back with my wife and family." David was clearly able to put the time in California away, into the past and into memory, but that turned out not to be true for the unmarried woman with whom he had become involved.

Within the boundaries of secrecy, if an affair endures it must develop a satisfactory practical dimension. Sometimes affairs also develop public ones. Any affair of some length has its own rules, customs, and habits that are like oil to its engine and are more or less satisfying to the participants. Under these rules, customs, and habits it develops a practical side. For instance, it became customary for Annie to cook a simple meal for her first lover; she also occasionally washed some of his socks. "I couldn't bear to see what a mess he lived in. He looked so uncared-for, and there I was, going home to look after my family. So I began to cook a little—not too much—and I washed some socks. Again, you know, not too much, but something."

Customs and habits evolved, both in bed and out, such as a light, jocular style of communicating and rules over what could be mentioned and what could not. These both sustained and defined their affair and enhanced the practical ease with which the affair could be conducted; indeed, it endured for a number of years. They met on certain nights but not others. They met at his place, never hers. She did not talk at length about her marriage or her children, nor did she probe about his life. They did not go places together or become friends with each other's friends.

The public aspect of an affair, even when secret, can also help to maintain it. Because they were in the same academic field, Jessica and Daniel were often together as colleagues, arguing over fine points, contributing to each other's seminars and lectures, and responding to each other's papers. This public face, the appearance that they were simply colleagues, was enriching, and it heightened their passion. Indeed, the fine line between the public and the secret lent an additional thrill: their affair was forbidden but was being played out almost, but not quite, publicly.

In unusual cases, however, affairs have both public and practical dimensions. Affairs conducted between colleagues and workmates can more easily encompass these other dimensions and even still remain secret. Cathy and Bruce's is a case in point. Cathy was Bruce's administrative assistant, and the line between professional and personal administrative assistance became easily blurred. Along with Bruce's professional appointments Cathy also made his and his children's social, medical, and dental ones, since Bruce's wife was partially disabled and these were Bruce's responsibilities anyway. While Cathy dropped off work for him, she also ferried his children around town. When they went on professional conferences, they also took vacations. In addition to her professional salary, Bruce helped her out with her mortgage and occasionally other personal expenses. Their public lives and the practical logistics of running these lives easily meshed and crossed the boundaries between the professional and the private. They were a good team in all four dimensions.

His Affair and Her Affair

In addition to the assumptions about marriage that underlie our thinking and conduct in affairs, there is another fundamental aspect that concerns the gender of the person having the affair. We all make assumptions about ways in which being a man or a woman informs both our experience and our expectations of sex, as we saw in chapters 2 and 3. Broadly these assumptions may be thought of in these ways:

1. One view says that men and women have different sexual needs. The assumption here is that women are more likely to be faithful because for them love and sex are inextricably bound. An example of this is the case of Ron and Norma. Ron was consumed by jealousy of an affair Norma had had in the distant past. He presumed Norma had been in love with the other man. Yet if Norma denied loving the other man (which she had done in private), she would have been even more damned. For both of these Irish-Catholic, working-class people, Norma's having a sexual relationship with a man she did not love was too unseemly and terrible: good

Catholic women, especially if they are mothers, simply do not have sex for the pleasure of the experience.

2. Another claim is that women are becoming more like men or that sex for women has become "masculinized." This means that if women are having more sex, they must be getting more like men. They are becoming more casual about sex and having more of it. This idea accounts for the results of recent surveys such as Shere Hite's, Blumstein and Schwartz's *American Couples,* and various magazine surveys in both the United Kingdom and the United States. These surveys suggest that women are now having almost as many affairs as men and, unlike in the recent past, are reporting that love and sex are not inextricably bound for them.

3. As we have discussed, there are male and female differences from the beginning. These differences emerge in men's and women's expectations in relationships and in how they behave. Because women may be having more affairs than before does not mean they are behaving more like men. And just because they tend to become emotionally involved does not mean they equate sex with love. Annie was emotionally involved with her first lover, for example. She felt tenderly enough about him to think about him when she was not seeing him and to worry whether he was eating enough. She was concerned enough about him to wash some socks and cook a little meal for him when she saw how he was living. But it was a question of degree: she knew she was not in love with him. She did not confuse her concern with love or her lust with devotion.

It is this third view that we take in this book. We believe that men and women act differently in affairs even if they are having them now with more frequency. We do not believe women's experience of sex has been masculinized. Women still show different attitudes and behavior in many areas connected to their affairs.

The difference between David, the husband of Ursula, and Annie in the way they thought about the effect of their behavior on their marriages and their affair partners tells much about differences between men and women. David was surprised when the woman from his California sojourn was angry that their affair ended for him when he stepped on the plane to return home. She had expected some follow-up, some word from him, some indication that he still thought about her. "She knew I was married," he countered, surprised by the ferocity of her reaction. "I told her about Ursula, my family, that we had an open marriage, all of that. I don't think she should have expected anything more. I told her Ursula was the most special person in the world to me. I question her right to her anger, but . . . " He shrugged. He thought she had shared his understanding about the implicit boundaries to their affair.

In contrast, Annie made everything as clear as possible to her first lover before they began their affair: "I was married. I absolutely would not leave my husband. I just had a child. I could not spend much time with him. And now that he knew the terms, was it going to be all right with him? Because if it wasn't I wasn't doing it."

Both these people talked of these affairs as *bounded,* not about love but more about pleasure, sensuality, and self-exploration. But the gender differences were consistent. Annie talked about being concerned that her lover understood exactly what she was offering. She did not want to be misunderstood, to seem to be leading him on, to be responsible for his pain. David believed he was letting his lover make her own decisions. Her pain was her pain, not his.

Men and women do not operate according to the same principles: they construct things differently; they apportion responsibility and plan the situation differently. They have different strategies to maintain the balance and boundaries of the marriage and the affair; they act and judge themselves along different dimensions in their attempts to maintain good views of themselves. Annie made sure her meetings with her lover occurred around the interstices of her family life—no spill-overs. She never saw him except on nights or days when a babysitter was available, and then not too often so that she would not be thought of as neglecting her family. David went off on business trips or had affairs when he was already away from the house on business. Since he was away quite frequently and Ursula was at home, he did not have to worry too much about whether the house was running smoothly without him. He had more leeway in conducting his affairs than Annie did. Annie had to think first about her family, which took most of her time and attention, thus severely restricting her availability to have an affair. David already had the freedom that comes from control over his own time since Ursula oversaw their family life. Considering how to manage the intersection of the affair and family life was not a major preoccupation for him.

Differences clearly emerge when men and women give accounts of how they have conducted their affairs, underscoring once again the basic differences between the sexes. Annie felt she had done the honorable thing as a woman by being completely open about what she could give and what she could not. She was taking care of her lover as well as herself and the others involved as a "good" woman should: "Now that you know all that about me, now that I've made the situation absolutely clear, is it going to be all right?" David, in contrast, assumed that a grown-up, smart, mature woman would be able to take care of herself and read the signs for herself, just as he would have: "She knew I was married." From their respective points of view, each behaved responsibly and used mature judgment.

Men and women use different moral reasoning and attach different criteria to what they report themselves doing. There are male and female filters through which each makes sense of the experience. These views of themselves reflect moral thinking processes that psychologist Carol Gilligan has described as coming from a "different voice." The voices emerging in these accounts are indeed distinctly either male or female, as discussed more fully in chapters 2 and 3.

In the next chapter we will take up the questions of who is likely to have an affair, the when and why, and what sorts of affairs people have. First we turn to a consideration of some additional issues that illuminate the experience of affairs: the place in them of sexuality, of intimacy, of risk-taking, and of jealousy, possessiveness, and guilt. Secrecy is central. In this chapter we want to consider its significance in the affair itself, while in subsequent ones we will look at its impact on marriages.

Affairs and Sex

For most people marriage is still the crucible in which they learn about sexual relationships. Marriage is the supposedly sacred vessel in which to have sex. Mostly within marriage, though increasingly before it, boys grow into men who learn to link their intimate feelings to their sexual ones, and girls grow into women with sensual appetites in addition to their need to be close to and loved by somebody. But obviously sex occurs outside marriage, for there are many affairs. Sex is a pivotal aspect of affairs and is central to our definition of them. If sex is not involved in outside relationships, however intense, a married partner does not feel threatened. Such relationships are usually permitted, while sexual ones are not.

In Bruce and Kay's sixteen-year marriage, Bruce's five-year affair with Cathy, his administrative assistant, was tolerated because Kay, disabled by chronic depression and illness, believed their relationship was platonic. She went further—she appreciated the relationship because Cathy also helped her out, ferrying her children to and from school, making appointments for them, and helping her with typing. Since she could barely get up in the morning, let alone worry about her husband and children getting through the day, she welcomed Cathy's connection with her family, despite the fact that Bruce spent more time with Cathy than with her, and her children seemed as much at ease and affectionate with Cathy as with herself. She accepted Bruce's going away with Cathy on ski holidays and their spending many hours on weekends playing tennis or swimming together. In other words, the other woman was as intimate in most ways with her husband as she was, if not more. Yet as long as Kay was assured by Bruce that there was nothing sexual in his relationship with Cathy, she allowed Bruce and Cathy all the time together they wanted, especially since it released her from many daily chores and burdens.

The revelation of outside sexual relationships has profound effects on all marriages except the few open ones. This is true even if the sex is perfunctory, unsatisfactory, and short-lived, although the briefness or dissatisfaction with it are often offered by the spouse as mitigating factors for the affair. The sexual element of the affair can be more or less central. But whatever the importance or delight in the sexual aspect of the affair, if there is sex, its revelation is a wound to the marriage.

Why should this be so? Why should the sexual dimension more often than the other three dimensions of marriage be the point of betrayal? In chapter 4 we discussed some of the historically based reasons for this: how the patriarchal roles of the Victorian marriage have been replaced by a marriage founded on intimate friendship and companionship, for which other intimacies have become more threatening; and how many more close relationships, including those before marriage, have become sexual so that there is a greater need to assert that a marriage is unlike any other relationship. The result is a marriage contract that, initially at least, places more emphasis on the sexual fidelity of the spouses than was perhaps true a generation ago. You can be friendly with others, spend time with them, harbor and even display special feelings toward them, share money and even live under the same roof with them, but you cannot have sex with them. Or so says the modern marriage contract. Therefore, to have sex outside marriage is to break that covenant and to call into question the very basis of present-day marriage.

All marriages evolve implicit additional basic rules. These begin, as Annette Lawson has shown in her research, with the ideal that "marriage is for everything." What is supposed to be special to the marriage is everything within all four domains—public, practical, emotional, and sexual. But of course other people cross into these domains over the years of marriage, encroaching on that specialness. Cathy shared all of Kay's domains in Bruce's life. In Tessa's life there have always been others, both men and women, who have been more emotionally satisfying and closer to her in understanding than her husband Craig. Laura's husband has never had a special place in either the public or the practical dimensions of their marriage; instead, various friends and lovers have taken what she at first expected would be his place.

People apparently make adjustments in their view of what is special about their marriage. For Tessa the public and practical dimensions of her marriage are what are sacrosanct. If another woman took over her role in family outings and upset the smooth functioning of their domestic partnership or took her place in their social circle, she would feel hurt and jealous. Craig, it must be said, does not share her marital assessment; knowledge of her affair would be extremely painful because for him marital sex is still sacred.

The redefinitions these people have made of what is sacred to their marriages are not the common currency of what defines marriage. The common definition of the boundaries of marriage, in which sex with another is proscribed, is the one on which we tend to fall back—especially if we are the one whose spouse has had the affair. Redefining that boundary of marriage is uncharted territory, apart from the few who tried to do so in the wave of open marriages in the late 1960s and early 1970s. But questions persist in these redefinitions: If one redefines marriage as most special in its public or practical or emotional dimension, how does one describe what sets it apart from other relationships that are also public or emotional or practical? Degree? Amount? Types of shared activities? Or simply sharing the same household? If you publicly remove the exclusive sexual bond the world supposes, how do you present this specialness to the world? In other words, marriage covenants that forbid affairs have a special hold because they are clear. In an unequivocal way they state exactly how one is special to one's spouse.

Insecurity, possessiveness, and a sense of betrayal almost always accompany the revelation or discovery of an affair. The insecurity arises in large measure because someone else has usurped the supposedly unique sexual role. The possessiveness stems from the indignation over someone else taking what is clearly stated to be one's rightful place in one's own bed. The sense of betrayal is about the secrecy and accompanying concealment and dishonesty that are often necessary for the conduct of affairs, but at bottom it is the betrayal of the marital vow of monogamy.

Moreover, men's sexuality, as we have seen, may predispose them to seeking variety through sex rather than intimacy. But, as we have also seen, both sexual satisfaction and intimacy fluctuate over the course of a marriage. There may be points, therefore, when men are vulnerable to having affairs. They have a natural capacity to segment or cut off. They may believe it is perfectly possible to have an affair that does not get in the way of other special aspects of their marriages, apart from sex.

Women may be drawn to affairs because they have learned about the separate worlds of the sensual and the emotional, and they think affairs do not necessarily destroy marriages. Again, given the fluctuations over time in satisfaction in marriage, they may also think they can get something from an affair that is different from what they are getting in their marriages, and it can be obtained without destroying their marriages. Tessa is a case in point: she claims she has a strong marriage even though she is having an affair.

But, given the fundamental expectations that marriage will be monogamous, intimate, and honest, secret affairs, if discovered, will result in insecurity, guilt, betrayal, and jealousy, though not necessarily divorce.

After discovering her husband Simon's affair, Susie lost nearly ten pounds in two weeks and was chain-smoking. "I wonder if I'll ever sleep again. I can't trust anything. I don't know what to believe anymore. I feel as if everything has just collapsed. Completely. A house of cards," she said. Round-the-clock support from friends, doctors, and even Simon got her through this dreadful period. But then bitterness and betrayal set in: "How could you? How could you do something with her and sleep next to me? How could you live with me and talk to me, knowing you were lying to me?" And insecurity and jealousy as well: "She was young and beautiful. I thought, 'I'll never be able to look at a twenty-five-year-old woman with long dark hair and long legs again.' I'll always think of his description of her lips—I read that in one of his letters to her. I'll hate full red lips forever. And all I could think of was how old I am and how young she was." Sex is central to the potential reaction of one's spouse on discovery. To expect otherwise is naive.

The Tie That Binds: Secrecy, the Forbidden, and Excitement

Most affairs are, and remain, secret. This is because there are very few open marriages, while the segmented and marriage-is-for-everything models promote clandestine affairs. The prevailing view of affairs as detrimental to marriage, even morally abhorrent, dictates that most people do not reveal them. Secrecy is at the center of most affairs, yet honesty is supposed to be at the center of most marriages. (In chapter 7 we will indicate some of the ways secrecy about affairs can be damaging to marriages, particularly when the affairs are revealed.) Yet the secrecy itself might be part of the sustaining power of affairs. Ironically, it seems that secrecy can be central to both an affair's life and its death.

The risk of exposure can be central to an affair's excitement. Doing something illicit or forbidden is part of what sex is supposed to be about, or at least that message often lurks behind our sexual development. Behind closed doors, in the backseats of cars, after dark, and in husky whispers—all speak to the forbiddenness of sex. Even marital sex is hidden from children, grandparents, and the neighbors.

The forbidden is frustrating, but it is also exciting. In adolescence, when we endure countless societal and familial constraints on having sex, petting, foreplay, and the lead-up to penetration can be among life's most exciting sexual experiences, even though intercourse itself may be unsatisfactory. Memories of groping in backseats or in bedrooms while keeping an ear out for parental footsteps recall frustrating but often exciting times.

There is none of that in marriage. Sex in marriage may be emotional and intimate and become technically satisfying, but it is familiar and is not forbidden. As we have already stated, familiarity can in time breed sexual stagnation. Affairs introduce the thrill of forbidden adolescent sex, sex done behind someone's back. It is no longer a parent's back that must be watched but a spouse's. In this sense it can be revitalizing and extremely exciting.

In addition, the risk of exposure can fill assignations with both urgency and shared complicity, which heighten sexuality. Sharing secrets can be binding. The thrill of the secret and the sharing of it can raise the importance of an affair. In discussing an affair she had with one of the contractors who was working with her on a house she was decorating, Susannah, a successful interior designer, talked about how she and her affair partner conducted themselves with perfect professional aplomb in front of their work colleagues. This enhanced the sexiness of their affair: they had a shared secret and were putting one over on everyone else. Moreover, they had to "wait until the coast was clear" to show their feelings for each other, and the waiting heightened the excitement. Feeling "naughty" about this also made sex more playful. The feeling of complicity in something that was hidden from both spouses and coworkers bound this couple even more tightly.

Illicit affairs can also be dramatic, especially if there are signs that exposure might be near. The threat of exposure, or a brush with it, might begin the end of an affair or lead it into a more anguished phase in which partners consider whether or not to end it. In her affair with the contractor, Susannah came close to exposure. Her husband suspected that someone else had been in the house while he was away on business. He began to badger her and scrutinized her for signs that would confirm or disconfirm his suspicions. At the risk of exposure Susannah hastened to cool her affair, but this only made her lover more persistent. "He whined. He sent an emissary, a friend, to try to get me to see the light. This was not too bright a move since I did not want anyone else to know about it. Anyway, he eventually cajoled me into one last time. And then another. It was nerve-wracking, and eventually the last time really was the last time."

In desperation her lover sent a supposedly anonymous note to her, pretending it was from a third party; in it he threatened to tell her husband about the affair if she did not consent to another assignation with him. Up until then their reunions had been bittersweet, tinged by an urgency because it would be their last meeting. When she received the letter, Susannah felt as if she had been thrown into a cold shower. "That was it. I was chilled to the bone. I was dealing here with something that might be a whole lot worse than I'd imagined." The affair was over for her: the thrill of the game disappeared when she realized how deadly serious it had become.

If everything in a marriage is to be shared, what cannot be shared may assume a particular sweetness: it is mine, not yours. This was the subtle attraction of Christina's first affair. Cooped up in her house for far too long while her husband streaked ahead professionally and, in general, seemed far more competent than she, Christina was desperate to create something of her own. In addition to her new niche in the dance world, she had her affair. Its secrecy was imperative, not just for survival of her marriage but also for her own self-importance: it was hers; it had nothing to do with her husband. "I didn't want to tell him for that reason as well. This was *my* world, *my* work, *my* affair."

The secrecy that breeds guilt, then, can be the very thing that keeps an affair exciting and important, and binds its partners together. In that sense the secrecy itself may be the very heart of secret affairs.

The Other Side of Secrecy: Guilt

There are gender differences in secrecy. The pressure to keep silent is great for both men and women, but women find it more difficult to split off or segment their feelings. The pressure to tell comes in part because they have a harder time putting away their thoughts and feelings about their affairs than men do.

There are also gender differences in guilt. Both men and women feel guilty about affairs, but men, being better able to segment their emotional lives, can cut off from this guilt. Women increasingly try to control their guilt by bounding their affairs. Melissa, a mother who said that her affair made her more cheerful and consequently a better wife and mother, said, "*When* I think about it, I feel awful. I try not to think about it. I should not be doing this to my husband—or, rather, I should not be risking his finding out and therefore hurting him. It's important not to think about it if you don't want to be consumed by guilt, really. It's hard not to. You keep very busy. That helps." But just as men have learned to cut off more easily, women, because of their development, have difficulty splitting off their emotions. Annie tried not to think about her lover when apart from him, but she couldn't help having visions of dirty socks.

Another source of the gender difference is, as we have noted, the double standard that still operates, although somewhat modified from a generation ago. Sexual women are still wanton while sexual men are acceptable. As a result men are less likely to forgive their wives when affairs are revealed than women their husbands. Women's advice columns cry out for patience, advising women to go to a marital therapist to discover the why of the affairs and to use the experience to heal their marriages.

The different responses of men and women are of course consistent with the developmental differences to which we have frequently referred. A man acts; his wife's lover, as competitor, must be eliminated. Action must be taken to eliminate the competition. If the competition has usurped his role too completely, the wife herself has to go. Annie was banished and eventually divorced, after revealing her pregnancy by another man (although she intended to have an abortion): "Another man's sperm creating a baby in my wife? Sorry—that's *it*—even if I have myself slept with my secretary and others." At least this is how it seemed to Annie.

A woman, in contrast, nurses, picks apart, and embraces her, as well as others', feelings. Susie almost starved herself to death; she was so distraught that she could barely contemplate eating for weeks after discovering Simon's affair. Yet she stayed. She and Simon underwent weeks, months, of grueling discussions, fights, and sleepless nights trying to understand, above all, "what went wrong." She considered the welfare, feelings, and fortunes of the family, including her spouse. She did not act precipitately. She followed the advice of the columns and stayed.

Women are more likely to be divorced if their affairs are discovered, while men are more likely to remain in their marriages. In addition, women also feel more guilt than men when affairs are revealed because of the pain and emotional stress they cause. While no one is supposed to cause distress, women are supposed to be emotional protectors, not purveyors of pain.

Open marriages circumvent guilt if the affairs stick to the marital contract. In segmented marriages guilt may be reduced: people often feel justified in pursuing something they think they are not getting from their marriages, especially if they feel they have tried but failed to do so. The problem with this model, however, is that the decision to limit the marriage is one-sided. It thereby goes against the spirit of openness and intimacy that are the prevailing assumptions behind most marriages. Guilt then arises around the fact that there is both secrecy about the affair and the private recasting of the marriage as a limited business. Susannah said her husband would not "fit into the box" she needed. He could not become more demonstrative or passionate, so she decided after years of trying to make him fit that it was better to accept the limitations of her marriage and satisfy herself elsewhere. Susannah feels slightly guilty that she reached this decision without consulting her husband, but most of her guilt stems from imagining the pain he'd have if she was discovered. As long as her affairs remain secret, she shields herself from guilt to a large extent.

In the marriage-is-for-everything model, people feel guilty while they conduct their affairs. In this model people are cheating on the marriage as they would like it to be; they have not given up on it; for them marriage is not limited. Therefore, they are draining from it energy, time, attention, and sometimes other shared resources such as money.

Laura has a segmented marriage. Guilt is not a strong component of her affairs, yet it is an issue that she faces when contemplating exposure. Exposure or discovery breeds guilt. At that point Laura would feel like a "scarlet woman" who betrayed her marriage.

Richard and Polly are in a marriage-is-for-everything marriage. After the exposure of Richard's affair, guilt has overwhelmed their marriage. Richard is repentant, Polly accusatory, their children her accomplices. Richard is an outcast, and the marriage continues to be drained by the affair.

Guilt may also surface when things other than the marriage suffer as a result of either a preoccupation with an affair or a diversion of energy to it. Children and work are the chief areas that can suffer.

Christina began to be afraid that she was not giving enough time to her children, partly because she kept adjusting her schedule to accommodate her affair. "I'm probably staying over in London too much. I never was apart from them before, except when they stayed at my mother's. I'm not sure that an affair is proper justification for staying away from my children," she said wryly. "But it's probably good for them—I was probably too protective before. I don't know."

Nick, an academic and the father of young sons, began to feel that his work was being neglected when his lover, with whom he had had a child, began to make unpredictable and increasing demands on him. Guilt about how his work was suffering, among other things, helped him to end the affair. "She was just too much. Too engulfing. Too much all the time. I couldn't get anything done."

For both men and women guilt operates as a pressure to disclose and to keep silent. Guilt seeks relief; it is a terrifically uncomfortable burden to bear. Many think, quite mistakenly, that confession to the spouse will bring about this relief. Consciously or not, guilt is always around when there is a secret affair in all but open marriages. The pressure to tell comes from the imagined relief of confession; the pressure to remain silent comes from the imagined consequences. In chapter 7 we will focus on the various consequences for marriage of confessing a secret affair, keeping silent about it, or having a secret affair discovered.

Affairs: Putting the Marriage at Risk?

Clearly, especially from what we have just said, there are risks to a marriage in having affairs. When we interviewed people in the course of preparing this book, we had an idea that people in affairs were risk-takers compared to people who did not have affairs. Risk-taking can be pathological, non-pathological, a conscious impulse, or an unconscious act. It seemed a possible framework into which we could fit people who had affairs. However, while it is true that affairs represent risk-taking, we found that many people having affairs do not, at the time at least, see themselves as taking great risks. They often deny risk-taking even while acknowledging that they are not playing entirely safely with their marriages (otherwise they would not be so secretive). They tend to acknowledge the full extent of the dangers before they begin affairs and afterward, looking back on them.

Annie, who had affairs when each of her children reached eight months of age and whose marriage finally ended with a fourth one, said, "I didn't really think about all the risks, the effects on my husband, all of that. No. I don't think I could have carried on if I had. *Now* I think back [on the affairs], and I just can't *believe* what I did, the chances I took." She is in her second marriage now. "I would never do that now. Never. I am fully aware of the risks, and I would never take the chance and do that to Jonathan [her present husband]."

Melissa, whose affair with a mutual friend of hers and her husband's made her, at least in the beginning, "cheerful" and consequently a "better mother," said that, although her husband eventually knew about the affair, she was mostly not aware at the time of the emotional risks she was taking. Indeed, despite her best efforts not to think about the possible unpleasant consequences of her actions, she did become preoccupied with the affair, and she feels, looking back, that she made her husband suffer even though he appeared stoic throughout. To have subjected him to that pain was risky. In retrospect, she questions her wisdom in having the affair. "Do I think I should have done it?" she asks rhetorically. "No, probably not. But then maybe things would have gone from bad to worse between us earlier if I hadn't. Now I have to live with knowing I caused him pain. I don't know. The affair was great while it was at its height. Magical. Very hard to know. But I guess probably I would advise against it."

Similarly, people are often aware of risks before they have affairs, in the stage of contemplating them. It is like thinking of going off the high diving board and being acutely aware that to take the plunge involves a number of near-escapes, potential disasters—so perhaps one should just climb down safely and not take the plunge.

Rita, a thirty-five-year-old mother of two, a doctor, and a writer, described her near-plunge: "I was in Boston visiting relatives when the nephew of one of their friends also came into town and was staying with them too. It was amazing—we were so alike. As soon as we began to talk, we found an immediate connection. It was an immediacy I had never felt with Donald [her husband of ten years]. We even looked alike! On our last night together we went out for a drink and ended up telling each other what we both felt. We kissed but then stopped. Then I had to really pull back—I just couldn't do it. Threatening my marriage, the stability of my life, my kids' lives. And I do love Donald. I just couldn't." She returned to Birmingham the next day. She still thinks about this other man, especially when she and Donald have their difficult and distant times, but she did not take the plunge. Instead she saw the dangers and "climbed back down again."

This notion of risk-taking, to distinguish those who have affairs from those who do not, is also complicated by the fact that although people do see themselves *post hoc* as having taken risks, others who did not have affairs, looking back over crisis periods in their marriages, saw staying in their difficult marriages as having been risky. Theirs was the risk of staying in what could and sometimes did become a dead and often painful marriage. However, those who have secret affairs are undeniably taking a kind of risk with the survival of their marriages, especially if the secret emerges, that those who stay in marriages, even troubled ones, do not take. It is a different kind of risk, actively doing something to change the status quo, the risk associated with any change. Because the affair is secret, it also puts at risk the implicit trust that the marriage is monogamous.

One notion is that this risk-taking is akin to daredevil stunts; the risk itself gives meaning and staying power to the affair. There may be something in this idea. During the height of the affair the negative accompaniments to risk-taking, such as anxiety, guilt, insecurity, and loss of predictability, do seem to become submerged. The positive aspects of risk-taking—the excitement, the thrill, and the headiness of unpredictability—are paramount. These are often decisive for continuing what is indeed risky, giving the affair a life and energy of its own.

"Whenever I found myself alone, unwatched at night, like out in the car on some errand, it was never just an errand but an opportunity to try to get a phone call through to her—that is, if it was also likely that her husband wouldn't be around. My heart would start to race as I got in the car. This must be how addicts feel when they are within scoring distance of their drug." Sam talked in this way about the thrill of breaking through constraints to phone Ellen, his old high school girlfriend. It was like the thrill of safely completing an obstacle course. Moreover, the anticipation of meeting and the plotting to arrange contact gave the affair an extra shared dimension.

The time and thought devoted to the execution and operation of an affair adds to its impact, as does the thrill of successfully negotiating risky courses and solving tricky puzzles. "There was a week when my lover's girlfriend was going to be away, and he could get a house by the lake for us for the whole week," Christina recalled. "I had to think of a way to get there. Staying overnight was out of the question, but luckily the house wasn't that far from mine. Instead of going to London, I just went there on two of the days. On the other ones I invented all sorts of errands and things that meant I couldn't do my normal routine. It was pretty hair-raising, but luckily for me it worked. The same with phone calls. It really was, 'If a man answers, hang up.' Again, luckily for me, I could go down the street and make a phone call from a public phone. But this took careful plotting and not very long phone calls."

The person having a secret affair has to be thinking about it an

inordinate amount since its logistics require so much time and energy to meet, when to do so, how to conceal the meetings or contact.
Such expenditure of effort, coupled with anxiety, means an attention to the affair that is often out of proportion to the feelings it
inspires. Such time and attention can themselves lead to an exag-
geration of a person's feelings about the affair: "If I am prepared to
spend this much time and energy, then I must have deep feelings or
it must be important." Alternatively, it can lead to an affirmation of
the affair, following an inevitable question, such as: "Do I really
want to spend all this time and energy arranging, concealing, worry-
ing? Perhaps I should give this up." If there is an affirmation of the
affair's importance, the commitment to it becomes strengthened.

When an affair begins to end, the negative accompaniments to
the risk become more salient. In this period a person feels the threat
to the marriage, the acknowledgment that secrecy from the spouse
is a betrayal, and the accompanying guilt and shame. This is the
time when the person most often feels guilt or shame, since earlier
the thrill acted like a shield against them.

When Christina's second affair began to end, because her affair
partner was threatening to tell his wife and end its secrecy, she had
to question whether she could continue "bending her life out of
shape" to continue seeing him. "And besides that, I had done something *really* bad. You don't bust up a friendship between two men—
one that had existed before I came on the scene. I really did
something awful. I couldn't let my husband find out about it from
him or anyone else." Its threatened publicity forced her to face the
effect of the affair on her husband and children. The confrontation
yielded enormous guilt and shame. Instead of affirming her commitment to the affair, she committed herself anew to her husband
and to family life. The thrills of the past felt like danger now.
Confronting her marriage's endangerment helped her to end the
affair. "I'll never get over it. They'll never talk to each other again,
but they have lives that keep intertwining. I also loved him very
much. It's all too terrible. Seeing that, I had to end it."

The risks stem from several sources. If the affair is secret, the
stability of the marriage usually depends on that secrecy being
maintained. But because an affair always involves two people, the
secrecy is not under any one person's control. It can be revealed

through the affair partner or through his or her friends, either wittingly or unwittingly. It can be revealed through discovery by a third party: Linda, for instance, found herself having to quickly invent an elaborate and scarcely believable story to cover up a lie. She told her husband, Peter, that she was with college friends on a day she had spent with her lover, Bill. However, a neighbor subsequently made a casual reference to having seen Linda and Bill together on the day in question. "We ran into him on the way downtown," she said, coolly covering up and implying that the friends were also around. Her innocence was maintained.

Stories of this type are legion. Often the attempts to salvage things through invention such as Linda's do not succeed. Partners have to meet to conduct their affair, so all affairs have a public aspect, which means that secrecy is never complete. A therapist colleague, checking into a resort hours away from the city in which she lived, saw a couple leaving. It was a married woman whom she had seen for therapy a year previously. She was with the lover she had supposedly renounced eighteen months earlier. This woman's secret was safe with our colleague, but others have not been so lucky. Similarly, any evidence—such as credit cards, diary entries, letters, phone bills with records of individual calls—can lead to the discovery of the secret. In Nora Ephron's *Heartburn*, a discovery of this kind confirms the wife's suspicion that her husband is having an affair, and this leads to the end of their marriage.

But there are other sources of risks. One of the most significant is a change in attitudes or goals brought about by the transforming emotional and sexual experience that an affair can provide. Even when both people feel they know what they want from the affair and are determined to bound and control the experience so that it does not interfere with their marriages, sometimes the experience overwhelms them. It goes out of control and leads to outcomes neither wanted in the beginning.

This is true in the case of Jessica and Daniel. They were lovers in graduate school. Daniel was married at that time but was in the process of leaving his wife. Jessica and Daniel had an intense, romantic, and deeply satisfying sexual relationship that ended abruptly when Daniel got cold feet and left. Jessica was devastated. Jessica went on to marry and Daniel married again, and they had three children each. Fifteen years later they reconnected; Daniel's job was in a field related to Jessica's, and he had moved to a nearby town. "I'd heard he was being considered for a job at the college nearby. Of course I had kept up with news of him over all those years. I didn't know if he had about me. I do now, of course. He had, if not quite as assiduously; at least he was eager to know about me. Soon after he got the job he was at a meeting I attended. My knees turned to jelly. We made warm and polite conversation. He asked about housing, prices, neighborhoods, all that. I could hear my heart pounding in my head as we spoke, but I'm sure I looked cool. It took a few months after he moved in and another meeting before we went out for a drink, and then I realized he felt the same as I did."

Professionally, they now had frequent legitimate reasons to meet. Both marriages were relatively stable, although Jessica's sexual relationship was unsatisfactory, and she and her husband were rather distant with each other. Daniel and Jessica began to see each other with no thought of leaving their marriages. Their occasional professional contacts led to more frequent social ones. Jessica's conscious agenda was to heal old wounds; Daniel's was to absolve himself of guilt. Jessica's unconscious agenda was to reclaim her lost love, and this, with the wisdom of retrospect, seems to describe Daniel's as well. In a few months they became lovers, as excitingly as before. Each tried to contain the relationship by labeling it as something special and extra to their marriages. Within a few months, however, Jessica's marriage was over, albeit also because her husband had recently begun an affair and wanted to end their marriage. Daniel's was faltering. Neither wanted to keep to the boundaries of something extra; both had come to resent the intrusions to their relationship that their spouses represented.

Sometimes discovery comes because of the spouse's reactions to the changes in the person having the affair. When Richard and Polly were married twelve years, Richard began an affair with a coworker. Richard and Polly had had two children, eighteen months apart, in the early years of their marriage. When the children were born, Richard was pursuing dental studies. The children became Polly's sphere while Richard lived increasingly on the fringe of family life: he provided economic security while spending very little time with his family. Nevertheless, his presence was expected and regular at particular times. He was around on weekends, for instance, and he did not leave for work before the children went off to school. Polly tolerated his minimal involvement as long as he stuck to familiar routines—helping out in the mornings and being there for weekend activities.

"It's true he was never around with the kids. No wonder they resent him now," she said bitterly years later. "But we managed. The affair was just the last straw." However, when Richard began his affair, he also began to break the routines. Occasionally he left earlier than usual. Sometimes he wasn't home for part of the weekend; once he stayed away a whole weekend. Sometimes he worked later than usual. During his affair he stretched the already tightly constructed limits of his family participation, and Polly could not tolerate his stretching them any further. These changes, stemming from his affair, provoked Polly to challenge him to be more involved with his family, even a greater involvement than before his affair. Her challenge precipitated Richard's confession of the affair and a crisis in their marriage.

"I know what I did was wrong," he said mournfully. "And it looks as if we'll never get over it." Even now, four years after the affair ended, they have still not recovered from their marital crisis; it is not clear whether they will remain married even though the affair is now long over.

Sometimes the risk to a marriage comes from the fact that the experiences in the affair lead to a different expectation of marriage and changed demands on the spouse. The difficulty is that these changes come about unilaterally; the other spouse has not undergone the same redefinition of the marriage. Since marriages have many aspects, any marriage can be redefined as needing strengthening in any number of areas.

From Bill, her affair partner, Linda received understanding, readily demonstrated desire, conversation, and appreciation, so she felt she could no longer tolerate her husband Peter's taciturnity, his infrequent praising of her, or the fact that he almost never told her he desired her. "Who was this person? I hardly knew him. Horrible. So distant. And I was so angry about his making unilateral decisions about his career, about his sleeping with that woman, about his not talking and my having to do all the talking for us, to get him to express things. . . . Only I didn't know it. The experience with Bill was like a big explosion. You really have to watch it. You *think* you can control things. You *think* you know what you want." However, when Linda began to ask for more—more talking, more praising, more telling her that he wanted her—he responded with, "What we have is normal. Men aren't like that." Linda could not counter with, "Yes, they are. I know one who is," much as she wished she could.

This couple was able to renegotiate their marriage with the help of a marital therapist and without Peter ever discovering Linda's affair. However, there are many couples whose marriages have ended. A fuller discussion of this will appear in chapters 7 and 8 when we talk more about the effects affairs can have. The point is that affairs can provoke changes in people—in the way they feel about themselves as a result of the affair, in the way they conduct themselves in their marriages, in the way they feel about marriage, and in the way they feel about their spouses. These changes may pose risks to their marriages.

Affairs and Intimacy

Clearly, many people derive a good deal more intimacy and emotional sustenance from their affairs than from their marriage, at least at particular moments in time. The case of Linda and Bill is an example. Linda had become distant from her husband, especially after she became a mother. Peter was the type of person who was comfortable on his own. Whole days could pass without more than a few words exchanged between them, and Peter would not have noticed. But Linda did, and she felt increasingly unhappy and lonely. When she began her affair with Bill, she felt a deep empathy, appreciation, vitality, and mutual desire in his company. Bill was warm, funny, and compassionate. Linda spent most of her free time with Bill, losing touch with many of her friends in the process. She had never felt so deeply in love, emotionally safe, and happy as when she was with Bill. Clearly this affair, despite its intensely painful aftermath, as we shall relate later, brought with it for Linda huge emotional rewards.

It is not only when there is a noticeable absence in marital intimacy that affairs can have such emotional impact, however. Christina's first affair gave her a new type of appreciation, friendship, and shared interests. She acknowledges that this coexisted with another set of activities, interests, and common values shared with her husband. "We shared London and the dance world," she said of her first affair partner. "We did not share a domestic life, children, a history."

As we have already noted, those people who operate with segmented models of marriages are those for whom marriage has some limits. We do not want to convey the idea that an affair for them is without losses or difficulty apart from the obvious one of risks to the survival of the marriage. Perhaps Sam encapsulated some of this when he said, "Each time that I have had to conceal something about my affairs I felt sad." This is especially so in the beginning of an affair, with the first concealments, and when one is emotionally affected by the affair partner or by things that happen in the affair, but one cannot, obviously, tell these to one's spouse. For Sam, who on the surface seems to accept that he is not going to be monogamous in his marriage, this concealment feels sad because it simultaneously "shows and increases the distance between us." Each letter stuffed into his briefcase, each surreptitious telephone call breeds more distance and further walls off intimacy. When his parents died, he shared his deepest pain with his lover. "Maybe I should have tried being more with Marlene. Maybe she would have understood more than I thought." He will never know. Their intimacy was by then already limited, increased by his affair, a process begun and sealed by a previous one.

When Linda went through the breakup of her affair with Bill, she could not share any of her intense pain with Peter, her husband. She suffered physical symptoms, even ending up in the hospital, so weakened was she by her suffering. Although she confided in a few safely distant friends, she could not tell her husband, paradoxically the one person with whom she was trying to become more intimate. This made the breakup from her intimate connection with her lover much more painful; during her mourning (which felt, especially in the beginning, very much like an extended "cold turkey") she often questioned the worth of enduring it, cut off as she was from the very intimacy she sought. She also, of course, had been unable to share her pleasure, her happiness, her sense of being alive again at the height of her affair. For both Sam and Linda their secret happiness was sealed forever from their spouses. To some, affairs may offer rewards, and they may appear to be a solution to marriage's many contradictions. For others, however, they multiply the problems. Even those who have an overtly open marriage can have difficulties managing the shifting boundaries between affairs and marriages. But before we look at the effects of affairs, in the next chapter we will look at who is more likely to have an affair and under what conditions.

6

The Who, Why, and What of Affairs

Be faithful darling, while you're away,
For when it's summer a heart can stray. . . .
If you go dancing and he holds you tight,
And lips are tempted on a summer night,
Your heart beats faster,
When the stars start to shine,
Just remember, darling, remember you're mine.

Pat Boone, 1957. Music and lyrics by
Mann and Lowe, Warner Chappell Music, Inc.

*P*EOPLE HAVE AFFAIRS FOR A HOST OF REASONS, BUT THERE are some factors that make it more likely. Whether or not people have an open marriage is obviously the most important, but there are others. These include the point they have reached in their own lives—young adulthood, middle age, or older, as well as the ages of their children, if any, and particular aspects of their own history and background. By this we mean each spouse's history of parental affairs.

Ursula and David, for instance, had had parents and even grand-parents who had carried on affairs quite openly. Their parents' friends had had affairs. Their marriage was, from the outset, an open one.

Predisposing factors for having affairs also include the strengths and weaknesses in levels of intimacy, how well a couple has negotiated issues of autonomy, and how satisfied each partner is with sex in the marriage.

In Sam's and Marlene's marriage, Sam had never been content with either their sex or intimacy. At the beginning of Christina's marriage, very little was separate. Only when children were born did a clear division between the couple evolve, and then it was without explicit negotiation between the couple, which set the scene for the couple's gradual drifting into emotional and sexual distance. The process culminated in Christina's private and secret decision to have an affair—one more slice of the newly independent and separate piece of her life.

Our research also suggests that the decision to have an affair and its impact will be different for women and men, for each comes to affairs, as they do to marriage, via different sexual and emotional developmental pathways. Annie's washing socks in her affair versus David's being able to step on the plane and end his affair are examples of this difference. This chapter examines the predisposing factors to affairs.

The open or segmented models of marriage promote affairs directly or indirectly, while the model that says "marriage is for everything" puts them way beyond the limits. Although some people have affairs just because they are forbidden, as we will see in our discussion, many are stopped by this interdict. In effect, then, the model of a marriage acts as a mind-set that influences both the likelihood of an affair and the way it will be played out. Models of marriage are not fixed for all time, however, and one of the effects an affair may have is to change the model.

Marriage over Time: Points of Vulnerability and the Marital Life Cycle

In the life cycle of marriage affairs are more likely to occur at certain points. There is no empirically based research to support this notion, but there are indicators as well as intuitive reasons for supposing that there are four primary points of vulnerability. The first point is in the early years of marriage, especially before children arrive.

When Kate was married to her first husband, she was unhappy and quite sure she had made a mistake. She felt that ending the marriage would not be simple, but the fact that they had no children made it enormously easier. She had married young and partly because she felt obligated to do so. She and her husband had been lovers as undergraduates, and their family and friends assumed their tightly dependent relationship would lead to marriage. But by the time they had graduated, begun graduate school, and moved out of the cozy surroundings of college life, Kate began to have doubts. By the time they actually married, she was sure it was all a "dreadful mistake."

Kate takes a long time to reach decisions, and she feels terribly bound by commitments she makes. "I should never have married him, but I realized that too late. I would have gotten out of it sooner or later, I'm sure. I just didn't know how. I met Jonathan through work. He was in a dreadful marriage, which was really over. Within a short time it became apparent we would leave our spouses. It was clear, really—just a matter of how and when."

She and Jonathan have been happily married for a long time. "Thank God we [she and her first husband] didn't have children," she said, glancing toward her two children with Jonathan as they played in the next room, and gulping as if to say, "Yes, that was indeed a close shave."

Having affairs in the early years of marriage might also be considered carry-over sexual behavior from premarital days, especially among those who had a number of premarital sexual partners. Linda and Peter lived together for five years; both had had a number of sexual partners before they met, and they believed it was "not right" to restrict each other sexually. Each had a number of affairs during the time they lived together. After they married, Peter continued to have casual ones, but Linda felt uneasy about that. She refrained from having any affairs until after their first child was born, and when she had hers, it was of an entirely different nature and nearly ended her marriage.

It might also be argued that affairs in this early period of marriage test one's commitment to the marriage or work out its boundaries, as the following story shows.

William and Nicola were among the first to marry in their social group. They were lucky enough to find part of an old rambling house to live in, with lots of space. The social life of their unmarried friends centered around their house and the parties they held. As William explained, "I think at the time—this was the late 1950s—we saw ourselves as a progressive couple. We joined in the social activities of our friends. At a party we each would dance with other people and sometimes flirt. Our rules said that kissing and maybe a bit of petting were okay but not sleeping with other people—at least when we were both around. We had a sort of understanding that if we were apart for a long time, no questions would be asked. Looking back on it, I think we were rather naive but also idealistic. Much of the time we behaved like our unmarried friends."

After five years it was perhaps inevitable that one of them would get seriously involved with someone else. Nicola decided she wanted to leave the marriage. "Separating hurt for a time, but it was relatively easy. We had no children and little enough property to divide. I think our families and friends found it more difficult than we did. They saw us as the ideal young couple. We were very young, but I certainly don't regret the time we spent together."

The second vulnerable point is when children arrive. When a woman becomes a mother, she often feels she has lost her sex appeal. When another man becomes interested in her sexually, it confirms that she is more than a wife, mother, general drudge, and Girl Friday, and it can be enormously seductive. When a man becomes a father, he may feel marginalized, pushed aside by his wife's preoccupation with the offspring, moved off center of the emotional stage, out to the wings, away from the intense emotional business between mother and child. When another woman becomes interested in him sexually, it confirms him as something other than a side issue in domestic arrangements and, what's more, interesting and appealing, and it can definitely be tempting.

It was no accident that Annie began two of her affairs when each of her babies was about eight months old. Each affair confirmed her sexuality. Most women find it difficult to shed the weight they gain in pregnancy, and this was true in her case. Nursing often makes a woman feel that her breasts are no longer erotic zones but simply feeding vessels. Exhaustion and post-birth tenderness means sex takes a backseat for many months. "Who was I, anyway, outside of this baby's mother? And mothers are definitely not sexy, are they?" Annie said. This was how she felt, and her husband, undemonstrative at the best of times, did nothing to counteract her demoralized state. It was a revelation to Annie that Joe, the man she met in an evening class, found her so sexy.

When Polly had two children in quick succession early in their marriage, Richard felt increasingly unimportant. Polly and he had met and married young, passionate about each other to the wedding day. Polly became pregnant almost immediately. Always a bit overweight, she gained an enormous amount during her pregnancies. Her interest in sex waned after her pregnancies and never returned during their children's early years. Always exhausted and preoccupied with managing two extremely active and demanding children, Polly not only showed little interest in Richard but the interest she did show seemed to focus on when and how he was going to be around to help her. "He was never there when we needed him. Hell, he was never there—period. The kids hardly knew him. I hardly saw him. We did go fishing and on a few camping trips. Things like that. But I did almost all of it by myself."

Resentment built up. They never could seem to recapture their early passion, and Richard spent more and more time away from home. A young dental assistant in his practice began to show an interest in him. She was fun. She enjoyed many of the same interests that he used to share with Polly but that she never had the time or energy for anymore. They went out for long walks, canoe rides, climbed mountains, and saw films together. She enjoyed him and admired him. Whereas at home Richard was seen as a nuisance, with his lover he was a king.

The third vulnerable point is when a couple enters middle age. A time of reflection occurs when a couple reaches the period of consolidation of both family life—when it is likely there will be no more children—and career development. Questions arise about whether the life you find yourself in is comfortable and desirable. This has been labeled a "mid-life crisis," but we we feel this is an overstatement of what normally occurs for everyone. There is ample reason to believe that, along with career and other identity issues and along with rethinking and prioritizing of values, what gets reconsidered are such issues as monogamy and the definition of one's marriage.

Nick, the proverbial mild-mannered academic, at the age of thirty-nine met a woman at an evening language class, began an affair with her, and set up a second family, unbeknownst to his first family. This second woman was entirely different from anyone he had known before, and he was overwhelmingly attracted to her. She was demanding and unstable but also passionate, in contrast to his dependable, cool, and undemonstrative wife.

If mid-life entails an appraisal of what does and does not fit with the years left to live in view, clearly it is a time ripe for beginning affairs. This appraisal in mid-life may focus aspects of oneself not currently expressed in one's marriage. An affair may well become the pathway through which new goals develop.

The fourth vulnerable point, and one that often coincides with the third, is when children leave home. Time on one's hands, without the common bonds of children, can expose gaps, even chasms, of interests and concerns between the married couple. It can simultaneously create opportunities to meet others and reveal emotional and sexual holes in the marriage. These are both reasons for an affair at any point in the marriage, and the combination of circumstances makes this a more vulnerable time.

Moira got married young to the first boy with whom she ever went out. When the youngest of her three children began elementary school, she returned to secretarial work. Fourteen years later, the last of the three children had moved away from home and she had risen to an administrative post where she was responsible for the day-to-day running of a small family business. She enormously enjoyed not only the work but the feeling of competence it gave her. But once the children left home, she felt restless. A recently divorced female friend asked her to go with her on a vacation to the Mediterranean. Moira had never been away without her husband and children, but with a little persuasion she went.

On the second night of the trip she was slightly shocked when her friend picked up a man in the hotel bar and spent the night with him. A couple of evenings later the friend set up a double date with him and his friend. "I suppose I knew when I agreed to go out with them what would happen, but it was a revelation to me when we slept together. He seemed excited by me, and to be honest, I was by him. . . . We spent the rest of the holiday together, but I decided not to see him when I got home. I knew it could not go on, and I don't think I really cared that much for him anyhow," she confessed. The homecoming had been only a couple of months before our interview for this book. When asked about her marriage and whether or not she would have another affair, she looked very thoughtful and said, "We'll see."

Particular Problems in an Individual Marriage

Because contemporary marriages must be both companionate and romantic, they are particularly vulnerable. They are supposed to be fulfilling on too many fronts and in too constant a fashion. If our ideology permitted a lapse in romance at, for instance, the time of having small children, with an expectation of a rekindling when children reached adolescence, perhaps more of us would accept the lapses that do occur in marital harmony. But instead many people end up feeling that their marriages have failed them; they become alarmed rather than patient and lose the perspective that the painful state will end and yield to another, more fulfilling phase.

Over time, even the best friendships and the easiest partnerships encounter times of difficulty or estrangement. Partners in a marriage in which friendship is the key may well grow apart in some ways while they remaining intimate in others.

Christina's marriage exemplifies this. Although in her estimation she and her husband were "mostly compatible," she felt that he could not share her work as a dancer, a dimension of her life in which she felt herself flowering. In the period of her life in which her first affair began, she felt quite alienated from him because of this. But if a marriage is supposed to be intimate in a consistent, stable, constantly upward trajectory over most (if not all) dimensions of friendship, even the "friendliest" marriages will be vulnerable. In Christina's case it was the dimension of her self-discovery. If you bring in the expectation of romance, which usually contains the expectation of sexual fulfillment, things become even more vulnerable. Christina felt very satisfied with her sexual relationship with her husband. However, hearing him say how beautiful she looked and how much he desired her had lost much of its luster, while hearing her new lover say it had not.

In addition, there are conflicting images of what is sexually stimulating. Sex is assumed to be fulfilling as part of a loving, committed relationship. But it is also exciting when it is new, forbidden, and spontaneous. Spontaneity may be hard to sustain as a marriage matures. Familiarity and routine, which are central to the domestic life and love that define most marriages, conflict with this aspect of sex. Again, Christina had satisfactory sex with her husband but exciting sex with her lover. "He saw me as I used to be, a young dancer, someone he had once admired from afar and now could have," Christina said about her first lover. "He was excited by *that* version of me, not the one I'd become at home over the years. I mean that's very exciting, you know? It was fantastic. Being desired so strongly, admired . . . "

Romance, of which sexual fantasies may or may not be part, also feeds on notions of spontaneity and newness. Thus it may also be in part our expectations about marriage that make marriages vulnerable over time, when newness and spontaneity are no longer the rule. A marriage can erode in any of these areas—the sexual, romantic, or any number of indicators of intimacy or friendship—and so become vulnerable to an affair.

All marriages suffer ups and downs when it comes to satisfaction with the amount of support given, with the ability to discuss things comfortably, and with the amount of time and contentment in shared activities. Additionally, the public, practical, emotional, and sexual aspects in any marriage are each variously affected, often adversely, by outside events. Over time any marriage will feel more or less deficient in one or a combination of these dimensions. Therefore, it can be argued, any marriage is vulnerable, at some point at least, to an affair.

If you take a marriage that is at a particularly vulnerable point in the marital cycle and that lacks at least one important dimension and give one of the partners in that marriage an opportunity to meet a compatible person with whom to have an affair, there is a propensity, if not a likelihood, that the partner will have an affair.

Personal Legacies

"I would never do to my husband what my mother did to my father." In these words Jane, a thirty-three-year-old researcher, talked about her lack of interest in having an affair. She has been married for twelve years to her former boss. Indeed, her own marriage technically began as an affair: her husband was still married to his first wife, although they had already agreed to divorce and were living apart, when he and Jane and met. Her mother has been married four times. During the marriage to Jane's father, she embarked on a long affair with her father's best friend, which broke up the marriage. In each marriage her mother had affairs, and in two cases married her affair partner. Jane can still feel the childhood pain caused by her mother's affairs from both witnessing her mother's upset when affairs went wrong and enduring her father's anguish over the affair that ended their marriage. She feels an affair "is a bad thing for a marriage," and she is quite sure her husband feels equally strongly. Their relationship began only when he was truly out of his marriage and looking for another stable relationship. Their marriage is organized partly around the strength of a shared belief in monogamy, shaped by the conclusion she drew from her childhood experience: affairs break up marriages and cause pain for all.

Others take a similar experience—that is, their parents having had affairs—and draw very different conclusions. Susannah's experience of her parents having had affairs gives her permission to have affairs in marriage and also a model of how a marriage can remain stable and happy despite spouses having affairs. The difference between Susannah and Jane is that Susannah's parents' affairs were benign experiences for her.

Others report that the unhappy experience of their parents' monogamy, especially combined with the change in sexual mores in their own sexual coming-of-age that enabled them to experience sex as a "good thing," pointed up the folly of monogamy. Nick, an academic, pointed out that his parents' relationship was arid in the extreme. There was a decided flavor of "sex is wicked" in the way he was raised. Moreover, his family suppressed demonstrativeness, and he grew up in an atmosphere of emotional sterility. He discovered the delights of sex when he was at college in the 1960s and found a way to feel alive and uninhibited for the first time. Knowing he could make a woman feel wonderful gave him an emotional connection with another. "What a revelation! I can't tell you what making love to a woman and having her respond—feeling so emotional—felt like to me. I think I would shrivel up and die without it. I know I would become severely depressed if I thought I would never have the opportunity of relating to a new woman sexually again."

This proved a sticking point in his marriage, for when his wife discovered his affair, she demanded an end to his relationship with the other woman. He agreed eventually to end that affair, since he had by then grown weary of his partner's insatiable demands. But at this point he realized that he could not face a lifetime of prohibitions against affairs. "I feel alive when I am forming a new relationship, and that has to be expressed sexually." It should be noted that Nick has no close male friends. He is truly terrified by the prospect that he might never form a new relationship again (with a woman). "I don't ever want to think I could end up like my parents," he said with alarm.

Nick and his wife have now worked out an agreement whereby he is allowed to have occasional brief affairs, but only when away and the other women must have no illusions about ongoing, deep emotional entanglements. In other words, it is now an open marriage with a clearly negotiated contract. His wife is allowed to have affairs, too, but she claims to be uninterested in having any. Nick so fears becoming repressed—and sex is the one area in which he is not inhibited—that he considers living under the dictate of monogamy, as his parents did, tantamount to paralyzing inhibition for him. Nick has affairs to ward off his fear of monogamy. Jane avoids them to contain her fear of a marital breakup.

However, others repeat rather than correct their experiences of monogamy and affairs. Susannah's case illustrates that, as does Alice's.

Alice, the writer who explained that it was her decision to remain monogamous partly because of her "long-term perspective" that things in marriage always change, also did so partly because of the example of her parents' monogamous marriage. "It is not that I thought they had the ideal marriage. I think it's more subtle than that. I think what allowed them to stay together was that they did not 'stray,' and they felt they could trust that the other was always focused on him or her. A friend who has affairs once described the person in whom he was sexually interested as being in the foreground of the painting, while the other, his spouse, faded into the background. That's what I think my parents always had, even when things were rocky between them. They were always in each other's foreground, and they knew it. I think that's very important. I expect that from my husband and think he should expect that from me. I don't want anyone taking my foreground."

For many, monogamy or affairs was an emotionally important theme in their parents' marriages; for others, what their parents did or did not do in their marriages was not important. It is significant that a powerful experience of either parental affairs or monogamy influences one's sexual marital boundaries.

The Impact of Cultural Practices

Jaime, of Latin American extraction but now a resident of both the United States and the United Kingdom, has intermittent affairs that are not emotionally binding but are "fun" and based on shared events and interests—women he has met at conferences and who enjoy food, wine, and sex as well. The boundaries are clear, and he feels he never leads them to think otherwise. These boundaries are of time and place as well as of emotions. They may share sex and evenings out while they are at the conference, for example, but when they part, the affair ends.

He shares this style with many Latin men, he claims. He does not feel it detracts from his passion for his wife of twenty-five years. As far as he knows she does not know about his affairs, but he is not sure, since she might not mention it if she did. He thinks she might have had one or two herself, but he does not want to know. If he dwelled on it, he would get upset. In some ways, he says, his culture permits having affairs, but not knowing about them.

Maria, also of Latin American extraction and a resident of the United Kingdom during her adult life, corroborates this. "I do not want to know if my husband has affairs. All of my friends in Argentina have had affairs. It is only the ones where the husbands found out or they found out about the husbands' affairs that the marriages did not survive. On an intellectual level, we are not shocked by the idea that marriages can accommodate affairs. It is dealing with it emotionally that is difficult and that can break up a marriage. But we do not expect not to have affairs. It is curious. In our culture there is a sort of expectation that it will happen. You just need to protect yourself and your spouse from its becoming public and ugly."

Maria went on to criticize the notion in her adopted country that marriages ought to be open, that couples should tell each other everything. "That is not necessarily what marriages are for, and I don't think that this is the sign of a healthy, loving relationship. I think telling can be a very unhealthy thing. Latin men and women do a lot of things separately, and there are some good things to be said for that. Their marriages are not so stifling."

But when couples change cultures and move to a different country, they can be particularly vulnerable to having an affair because an intense relationship with someone from that new culture may help them become acculturated. This may be the case when one member of a couple gets very involved with the new culture while the other remains steadfastly rooted in the old. Or it can happen out of loneliness: one member of a couple might have a job that takes his or her energy and time away from the spouse, who may then feel very dislocated and lonely. A relationship with a new man or woman, particularly from the new culture, may help the lonely spouse ease into his or her new life, despite the frequently absent spouse.

Gender and the Impulse to Have Affairs

Cutting across all these factors and influencing them is the gender divide. The points of vulnerability in a marriage will be experienced differently by men and women. A fundamental difference is that when there are children, the woman is a mother and the man is a father. Motherhood and sexuality are often at odds with each other: mothers are not supposed to be sexy and they are also often too tired for sex. In addition, a woman's experience and expectations of marriage are different from those of a man. Thus, the vulnerability in risking the marriage or exposure by having an affair are different for women and men. They have different reasons for and predispositions toward having affairs.

Women generally have less powerful positions in the world of work and politics, and they still do much more at home. Recent studies about the shifting duties of men and women show that women, whether they work or not, assume most of the family and domestic tasks and responsibilities. This establishes conditions in which they can easily feel both undervalued and resentful after a while in their marriages. "I know that he thinks he works so very, very hard. He does. So do we all," Alice commented when explaining how she has at times deeply resented her husband. "What he doesn't realize is that I'm the one who clears away the coffee cup he doesn't even remember leaving on the desk two days earlier, that I make the children's dental appointments, that I take them to their music lessons and pay the teachers' bills, that I call up the other mothers—not the fathers, by the way—to arrange their social engagements, and so forth. *And* I take care of the cleaning lady. Even the work I don't have to do anymore I oversee. And I still write my books, go to my meetings, do my research. And he complains when the house looks filthy—which it rarely does, by the way. He complains if the kids are late to one of the appointments I've arranged. He complains about my out-of-tone body. Okay, he gently teases me about it, but he's making the point he's dissatisfied. Am I superwoman? Does he have the slightest idea of all I do?"

Under these conditions women can become vulnerable to another relationship that may restore flagging self-esteem. "I sure as hell appreciated it when Joe [her lover] told me how great I was in bed. You'd better believe it! He thought I was hot stuff. I'm glad *somebody* did!" Annie exclaims ruefully.

Men, on the other hand, may want to remain central to their wives and families, but too often they become peripheral. This establishes conditions in which they can easily feel remote, unnoticed, and unappreciated, which in turn creates a vulnerability toward women who confirm their attractiveness and importance. "The fact that this terribly exciting, passionate woman wanted me—me!—was incredible. How could I resist?" said Nick, recalling the beginning of his affair. In other words, men and women, in general, have different complaints about married life and so are vulnerable to affairs for different reasons. Men may complain that their wives are not sexy enough. "Ever since the children came, things have been different" has been said time and again during interviews, especially by men. They say their wives don't understand them, by which they seem to mean that their wives are no longer as interested in focusing on them and their shared interests as they were before they had children. On the other hand, women say they "cannot communicate" with their husbands and that their husbands do not seem to value them anymore. They also tend to feel more exploited, whether sexually or otherwise. Different patterns of development of their emotional needs, strengths, and weaknesses and of their sexual behaviors and attitudes explain much of these gender differences. So does the divide between them in societal terms: domestic and economic differences mean they face different social and economic risks if their sexual affairs are revealed or if their marriages falter or split.

When an affair is revealed, the marriage is more likely to be at risk if it is the wife's affair. Old-fashioned double standards combine with the gender dynamics of marriage to make the price of affairs higher for women than men. We shall explore this further in chapter 7. For now it is enough to point out that women are not usually as good as men at separating love and sex. They may invent "love" more often to justify affairs. Even if they do not call it love, they may take their concerns about their affair partners very seriously and dwell on them so that these thoughts spill over into their domestic lives, with distractedness or short tempers resulting. These ongoing concerns or intensified emotions then create conflicts between their affairs and their marriages, and they have to live with these conflicts.

When Annie had her final affair, she told her husband because she had accidentally become pregnant by her lover. This affair was a holiday fling, unimportant because she felt she had been treated in a cavalier fashion by her casual lover. It is unlikely it would have come to light if she had not become pregnant or if she had terminated the pregnancy without telling her husband. She thought, however, that her misery over the episode and her moral dilemma over an abortion might inspire her husband's sympathy and jolt him into showing that he cared. Instead her husband turned it all against her. He never knew about her first two affairs, but he leveled the latter ones against her: the first one he knew about, in which she fell in love, threatening their marriage, and now this one, in which she acted "like a whore, becoming pregnant by another man she didn't even care about." How much was he supposed to take? He left, and the marriage was over. Her final, unimportant, "just sex" affair precipitated the breakdown of their marriage.

Generally, men are more likely to have the opportunity to have affairs. They have more mobility and more chances to meet other women. Even if wives are working, men usually have fewer demands from home and therefore more freedom. Women may seldom get out to meet other men, especially if there are young children, while men are freer both to begin and to carry on an affair.

During her thirteen-year marriage to her high school sweetheart, Sharon felt little sexual desire for her husband. She had had one affair during an enforced separation early in their marriage. It had nearly destroyed their marriage. They went on to have three children. Sharon did not work outside the home, but as soon as the youngest child went off to school, Sharon took a part-time job. She found some time and freedom of her own, and within months was having the first of a series of affairs. "I feel terribly guilty about it. I should want him, but I don't. The sex with those other guys was just so much more exciting. I'm ashamed but I love sex. When an affair ended, I vowed it would never happen again. Then I'd think about life going on like this, without my desiring my husband forever and yet my not really wanting to divorce, and I'd get very depressed. Then we would have fights and we wouldn't have sex for a while. Then we'd make up and have sex, which is okay but dull, dull, dull.

"Now that I'm working, I eventually meet someone, and it all starts again. And I'm also angry that I can't seem to get it all in my marriage. Why is he so unsexy? Why does he have to be so straight and proper all the time? Maybe it's because these are affairs that they are so sexy. . . . I don't know."

Indeed, a common reaction from a woman on discovering a husband's affair is, after feeling hurt and betrayed, envy and anger: envy that he got there first and anger at the inequality of opportunity that allowed him to have an affair when this had felt closed to her.

When Matthew's wife found out about his affairs, apart from her shock, betrayal, jealousy, and hurt, she envied him his opportunity. "I'd been dutifully running our house, keeping myself attractive for him and only him. There had been opportunities—in fact, a great love from my past had persistently been after me—but I'd tuned them all out. I wasn't on the lookout. Maybe men had been interested in me and I didn't even know. Who knows? Matthew was playing by a different set of rules. Maybe I should have been playing *that* game, you know?" She was left feeling unsexy and unappreciated. She wondered if she was foolish to have been so oblivious to other men's attentions all those years.

Personality: Is There an "Affair-Type" Person?

The question remains: Why do some people have affairs and not others? Plenty of people are in unsatisfying marriages, have the opportunity, are at a vulnerable point in the marital life cycle, yet still do not have affairs.

Various attempts have been made to explain the differences in terms of personality. If one starts with the view—as many have— that affairs are, by definition, pathological because they are ways of consciously or unconsciously acting out against the marriage, people who have affairs *are* acting pathologically. In this view they are variously deemed immature, narcissistically disturbed, and sick. From such a perspective these labels may seem to make sense: people are not being direct, responsible, or "adult." But this is not only too judgmental, it is also far too simplistic.

There are other explanations. One is that those who have affairs are people who will take risks. But as we discussed earlier in chapter, this notion does not distinguish those who will from those who won't. Nevertheless, the view persists. Seen romantically, this explanation makes people who do seem creative and avant-garde. Of course, they may also be potentially destructive. Certainly this would be the view from the standpoint of those who believe that marriage is for everything. Risk-takers are people who cannot commit themselves or are unable to see the potential consequences.

Strength of religious belief or commitment to the ideals of monogamy also do not necessarily differentiate between those who have affairs and those who do not. Survey after survey shows the same result: that monogamy is almost everyone's ideal. As an ideal it has grown stronger and more widely held in recent decades. However, more and more people are having affairs. Churchgoers do not seem to have fewer affairs than non-churchgoers. What people say they should do ideally and what they actually do are different things.

There is some evidence that those who have had more sexual relationships before marriage are more likely to have relationships outside marriage. The rise we see in extramarital sex may be partly because there are now more married people who had more partners before marriage. While this may be statistically true, it does not explain why Mary, say, who had five premarital partners and is in a rotten marriage, forbids herself to have an affair, while Susan, in almost the exact same circumstances, draws on her past sexual happiness and confidence to have an affair in order to make herself feel rejuvenated.

Affairs and the Need to Retaliate

Some people have affairs because their spouse had one. The motive is to pay back, to hurt as you have been hurt, or to regain a balance of power. Or it may be envy. Or it may be that one's spouse's affair gives the other spouse permission to have one. It may serve both of these ends.

Ursula began her affair with Sean partly because her husband David had been having affairs. Their open marriage called for her to have an affair since it associated the ability to do so with a kind of personal growth. David encouraged her affair, and she waited for the right opportunity, person, and time in her life. She needed someone who was interested in having a limited affair with her, someone who was not too much like David, who shared with her something David could not, and who appeared when her children were older. "One of the most important things on which David and I agree is that we would never have an affair with someone who is too like the other. That would be taking away from us. So Sean is an artist. He is someone I relate to very differently from David. He doesn't compete with David at all because of that. I also just couldn't find anyone who was, you know, right before. I'm sure some of it was that I was just too busy and preoccupied, physically drained. But there had to be the right person. I'd had my eye on him for a while. I didn't know if he was interested at first. It took a little time. That was okay. Then we finally worked out a weekend away in Paris. David was with the kids. We planned it very carefully and looked forward to it for a long time. He was so excited for me. And it was lovely. Just lovely. Very poetic. Very romantic. Lots of kissing."

More often than men, women get rude awakenings from attempts to equalize or to pay back. Because it is more difficult for many women to segment their sexual and emotional lives, to cut off a set of emotions for one person from a similar set for another, they have more difficulty in keeping to the purpose of this type of affair. In Linda's case she fell deeply, passionately in love with Bill, although she began the affair because her husband had had a casual affair a few months earlier and she wanted to equalize the sexual power balance in the marriage. She thought that, like her husband

Peter, she could segment her affair and her marriage and, in doing so, strengthen her marital position. What she did not expect was that she would fall as deeply in love with Bill as she did.

"I may be a sucker for someone so in love with me. It was an explosion!" After it was all over she ruefully accepted that while Peter might have been capable of segmenting, she could not trust that she could ever cut off again. "Do I regret it? I can't say that. But I *can* say I *never, never* want to go through that kind of pain again."

Melissa and Lawrence were able to get the marital balance back again through a retaliatory affair. Lawrence had an affair with Barbara, a mutual friend, after discovering Melissa's affair with Max, another friend. "I don't resent his affair. I had drinks with Barbara's husband while it was going on—he knew, too—and he tried to get me to express my anger and pain. But I didn't feel it. I took it for what it was. There was nothing threatening about it. She wasn't going to go off with him or he with her. He wasn't in love with her, just intrigued by her. I can understand that—she's a little strange, you know, a little disconnected. He was doing it, in part, because we all were, and I had. We stayed friends with them for a while, but it was always a little awkward, and we've drifted apart." At the end of both affairs the balance of marital power was equal and familiar again. Lawrence's retaliatory affair worked to maintain balance in the marriage. Although his affair was not covert, it was not flaunted or endlessly discussed either. Melissa was reassured when it ended, but she had never really been worried.

Such rebalancing probably does not occur often, even if that is the intent. The effect often completely misfires when the motivation is primarily an eye for an eye. When the partner who had the first affair feels guilty, for instance, there is often a sense of relief when he or she finds out the other partner is having an affair. It lets the first partner off the hook. This may not be what the new affair is intended to do.

Another often undesirable outcome is that the new affair is seen as a worse offense because the partner let it happen knowing how painful its effects could be (from his or her own experience). This was one of the charges leveled by Annie's husband: "Along with everything else, how could you do this to me when you know what it feels like since I told you about mine?" Or Matthew's wife, who had had a brief affair early in their marriage: "He suffered during that time. His pride was hurt. I promised it would never happen again. Nothing was worth what we went through at that point. So then *how* could he do what he did, knowing how it felt? *How?*"

The Pull of "Unfinished Business": Settling Old Scores

Affairs may begin because of unfinished business. That is, old lovers, even ex-spouses, or old friends or colleagues who were attracted to one another but who did not act on it or old crushes who suddenly declare an interest—all of these have extraordinary seductive power and can precipitate affairs. This power stems largely from the unfinished character of these relationships. Either there is the need to become the victor, if one has been rejected, or to relieve oneself of guilt, if one was the person who walked out. Both needs may pertain in the case of past loves or former marriages. Or there may be a need to discover whether the old feeling is still there, especially in the case of past loves or old crushes and attractions.

Jessica spoke of this when she said, "I will always see him as a young boy, and he sees me as that young and passionate girl." If this is coupled with other things, the seductiveness grows even stronger. For instance, if you are going through a stale sexual period in your marriage and are also feeling middle-aged, that life is starting to pass you by, you might be particularly vulnerable to fantasies of getting together again with an old flame. Meeting that same person years earlier, in the days of the still-new and exciting marriage, might not have exerted the same seductive power. There is also the feeling that in a way you are not transgressing marital vows; the person who had been there first—the college love, the high school sweetheart, the first spouse—has some prior claim.

Daniel and Jessica are a case in point. When they met again, both were in marriages that had begun to feel distant, even "dead," in Jessica's case. Both were nearing forty. Jessica's husband commented, "I'm only an interlude between Daniel 'version 1' and

Daniel 'version 2,' anyway," when he was told about the affair, thus confirming that sense of prior claim.

In Margaret Atwood's novel *Cat's Eye*, the heroine, now remarried, on a visit to Toronto sleeps with her first husband, with deep familiarity and some affection. Although she is married to someone else, it does not feel like "adultery." Yet in their relative youth she had begun sleeping with this first husband illicitly before their own marriage, when she was the girlfriend of someone else. During that earlier phase of their sexual relationship, she did feel like an adulteress, betraying her boyfriend of the time with the man who was to become her first husband.

There is sometimes a confusion of time and place in affairs of this sort, with the earlier time seeming better, for it was a time of younger, often less complicated days. "To me he always looks like a young boy," says Jessica of Daniel. She feels connected with her old self, the younger girl she feels herself to be at times, through being with him.

Sometimes an affair can become a long-term sexual friendship. Gordon described a relationship that had begun some years before his marriage with someone who was a student with him. They went out together for a few months, and although they got along very well together, it was not a very intense relationship. They met again by chance a few years later. Both were then married, but they found a lot to say to each other. Gradually a pattern emerged in which once or twice a year they spent a couple of days and nights together. Sometimes the demands of their separate lives—and in her case a divorce and remarriage—interrupted the pattern but did not end it. Neither ever thought seriously of settling together, but also neither saw any reason not to continue the relationship.

The Oedipal Affair, a Variant of Unfinished Business

Wendy's father was the director of a company with a number of foreign offices. After she had been married for five years, she and her husband went to live abroad, and she started to work in one of the offices. One of her father's partners frequently came over to oversee the affairs of the company. He was very courteous and always took her out to wonderful restaurants while he was there. Sometimes she returned from their glamorous dinners unable to sleep, so high was she from the buzz she got in his presence. Then her father got sick, and the couple returned home. In the midst of untangling a lot of his business affairs, she turned to her father's partner for advice. Shortly after her father died, they met again at a social function, and within a few months they had begun an affair.

Wendy's greatest admirer had been her father. She and her mother had an embattled relationship, and the family was polarized: Wendy and Dad formed one coalition, her sister and mother another. Secretly Wendy suspected her father had preferred her to her mother. It was no secret to anyone that Wendy preferred her father to her. From adolescence Wendy had known that she was attracted to this partner, "I'm not a dodo. I realize he was a father figure, but he was so magnetic," she reflected.

They conducted a clandestine affair for five years, during which time her marriage barely survived. "It just pointed up so much that was wrong and boring with Jimmy [her husband]. That's how it got in the way. I felt I wasn't in love with Jimmy anymore. I was in love with him [her lover]." The affair ended when Wendy finally realized that she would never be able to marry this man. He had no intention of leaving his wife of thirty years, whom he still loved. Wendy was perfectly aware of the Oedipal-like nature of her relationship. She knew she was attracted to older men—and continues to be— especially men who remind her of her father. She was also aware of the thrill she got from knowing she was having an affair with the man behind her mother's back and behind his wife's back. His wife, of course, was old enough to be Wendy's mother.

Gene and Ann are eighteen years apart—Ann is forty-eight, and Gene is thirty. They met when Ann's marriage to a man of her age was deteriorating. Ann's elder daughter is two years younger than Gene; her younger daughter is six years younger. Five years ago Ann and Gene became lovers. Gene, Ann, and her two daughters lived together until recently when Ann's younger daughter left home. Gene's mother is an undemonstrative woman whose husband was rather weak and remote. Ann's now ex-husband, an alcoholic and a womanizer, treated her badly throughout their marriage. Ann is emotional and warm, while Gene is the cool, dependable one in the relationship. Although Gene is ambivalent about staying with Ann, partly because he may want children at some point, he feels intensely drawn to her and protected emotionally by her; moreover, he gets satisfaction from acting the dependable, strong man for her.

Life Traumas: Affairs as a Response to a Reevaluation of Life

George, a university professor of sociology at a major university, had a wife and two children. He had known his wife from adolescence, and they had married before he obtained his degree. At thirty-five he was diagnosed as having a brain tumor. During the months of hospitalization, outpatient treatment, and inactivity, which fortunately ended with his complete recovery, he spent a lot of time musing on the meaning of life in general and of his own in particular.

During this time he crystallized several of his vague notions: that he did not love his wife, although he was fond of her; that if he were to live, he wanted to study how people thought about the meaning of their lives, rather than what he had been studying until then; and that he wanted to live more passionately, with more feeling. A few months after his recovery he met a woman through his research, a woman completely different from his wife—dark where his wife was blond, intense where his wife was cool, confident and assured where his wife was diffident. This woman wanted George, pursued him, and with little effort won him. She, too, was married. They were lovers for eight years, until she ended the relationship. George remained married for three more years, until his children left home, but he no longer had a sexual relationship with his wife. During those three years he searched for another passionate woman; after finding her, he left his wife.

Following serious illness or trauma, such rethinking of life—its meaning and what one really wants to achieve before it ends—especially if it occurs in middle age, can become a catalyst for an affair. A life change can also bring this about.

In Matthew's case the significant catalytic life change was losing his job at the age of forty-three. Without a job or job prospects, Matthew became depressed. Losing his fancy cars, expense account lunches, and business-class travel was not an easy proposition for him. Depression sapped his zest for family life as well. On a trip to a job interview he met an unconventional woman who hotly pursued him, turning his life around in the process. As a result he left his family and at least temporarily suspended his life as a middle-class professional, trading it in for that of an aging hippie–world traveler. The loss of his job indirectly changed his life since he traded in one identity for another, in the company of the new woman in his life.

The Affair as a Compulsion

Some people seem unable *not* to have affairs. They are unable to relate to others of the opposite sex *without* sex. This is more common among men than women. This should not be a surprise, in the light of what we have been saying about differences between men and women. Intimacy does not come as easily for men as for women. If men are going to have a problem in forming close relationships, it is likely to be because they find it hard to be intimate. In more severe cases they distinctly fear becoming too close to someone. Because men's sexuality develops first in isolation and only later becomes blended with intimate feelings, it is also not surprising that men can have "just sex." Separating sex in this way, afraid of intimacy, more men than women are likely to seek sex with lots of people. Because having sex is having a kind of relating, it gives these men (and sometimes women) the feeling, however fleeting, that they are making some connection with someone. So, briefly, it establishes a sense of independence from one's spouse: "I have others, not just you."

Mike, an accountant, was married for five years. During that time he had many affairs, usually with women he picked up at bars or on business trips. His wife did not know about them. He was an alcoholic, although recovering when interviewed, and allegedly it was his alcoholism, which meant that he was frequently drunk and his behavior erratic, that eventually drove the couple to divorce.

As a child Mike had lived sometimes with his mother, sometimes with both parents, and frequently with his grandmother. Alcoholism ran through his family. His father was a hopeless drunk, his mother was an intermittent drinker, and their marriage was off and on. There was very little he could depend on, he said, which made it hard for him to trust anyone or anything, and in particular one woman. He also pursued women when he drank. As soon as he married he felt smothered. He is not sure why he ever married except that his wife was pregnant, they were at the age when they "should have been married," and it was the expected thing to do. But Mike had always been promiscuous and was always looking for the next "girl to get into bed." Sex and drink were like sedatives to him—ways to escape feelings of pain and distrust. He could not be long with anyone in case the conversation turned serious, so he was rarely home. Instead he was out at bars, at meetings, running around, and often ending up in bed with someone whose name he only dimly recalled. The constant sex with someone new acts as a protection against being too intimate with one's spouse. The affair partners are not usually emotional competition for the spouse, since the engagements are both transitory and superficial; there is always the next conquest to look for after this one has been made. In this way intimacy with the affair partner is avoided as well.

For many men there is also the fact that maculinity is affirmed through sex. The belief is that the more women who succumb, the more masculine one is. This belief is based on accepted cultural messages. But having sex with many partners does not confirm a woman's femininity in the same way. Fear of intimacy is not usually a woman's problem. When a woman shows this sort of compulsive sexualizing of relationships, it is usually a sign of deep pathology, since it clearly goes against normal developmental patterns. Men, too, may have a pathological need for sex; it is just not as likely to be defined that way, no matter how compulsive or destructive.

Some people have labeled this sort of behavior "sexual addiction," comparing both the "fix" that casual sex gives and its compulsive nature to genuine physical addiction. In these ways it is analogous. Sex in this way does protect against intimacy, and it does confirm that someone finds you attractive. For many people it is also intensely exciting and pleasurable because it is doing something forbidden. It offers a "fix" in the same way that drugs do, but of course it is not an addiction. There is no real physical dependence, and "withdrawal," though perhaps psychologically as intense as "cold turkey" or other addiction cures, is not physically painful or dangerous.

It often does not work in the long run, however. Because of its frequency, many risks are taken with one's marriage. Since many of the players end up feeling exploited, this type of affair often results in severe distress. Some spouses turn a blind eye, accepting that their partner has "a problem." But not all do. And in the age of AIDS there are new risks as a result of compulsive affairs. In these ways such affairs are riven with dangers, if temporarily palliative for those having them.

In summary, there are particular vulnerabilities in the course of any marriage because of people's own histories, and these contribute to why some people have affairs. One may be at a vulnerable point in the marital life cycle. Another may have a marriage that has become eroded in an important way. Some women may feel unable to feel close to their husbands or unable to communicate with them or feel overworked in comparison to them. A man may feel peripheral to, unappreciated by, or undervalued by his wife and family. Combine these factors with opportunities to meet people with whom to have an affair and the time in which to have one, and a spouse might well be on the way to having one. And if this scenario does not apply in a specific case, it does in hundreds of others.

7

The Impact of Affairs

Love, oh love, oh careless love,
Love, oh love, oh careless love,
Love, oh love, oh careless love,
See what careless love has done.

Traditional Blues

*T*HE IMPACT OF AN AFFAIR CAN BE POSITIVE, NEUTRAL, OR DIS-astrous. Or it may be a mixture of these, depending on whether an affair is secret and never discovered, whether secret and then discovered, or whether it was open from the beginning. There can be effects on the marriage, on the people having the affair, on the spouse or spouses who are not, and on others indirectly involved.

How to gauge the impact is impossible to summarize. There are a number of separate questions: Have there been changes in the expectations of the marriage, the sexual relationship, or satisfaction with intimacy and friendship? Generally, has the marriage improved, remained the same, gotten worse, or ended?

All of these potential effects, from the specific to the general, indirect to direct, and on whom are influenced by whether or not a secret affair remains secret or, in open marriages, whether an affair is conducted within specified boundaries. If an affair is secret and then becomes known, the impact of discovery itself is enormously important. For this reason we will look separately in a later part of this chapter at the impact of a secret affair after its discovery. First we will discuss the impact of secret affairs that remain secret and affairs in open marriages that remain within contractual boundaries.

In addition to the broad range of possible effects there are two major underlying issues that we need to deal with first: the way the gender of those involved influences the outcome and how this links to the model of their marriages.

Gender and the Effects of Affairs

In view of what we have already said about the development of men and women (see chapter 2 for a discussion of the different social consequences for each of marital breakup), it is not surprising that men and women report effects of their affairs differently. The differences are in both degree and kind.

On the whole, women still become more emotionally involved in affairs than men. This involvement is no longer confined to being in love. For most women, especially as they become more sexually sophisticated partly through their marital experience, the correlation between sex and love has loosened. Women now do not have to think they are in love to have sex. The issue of affairs can no longer be seen as "women are monogamous while men are polygamous." Women have affairs that do not involve love, but they usually have affairs that are emotionally involving. Because men can "cut off," given the clear emotional boundaries often demanded of them, they can have affairs that have minimal effect on their emotional lives. Even when men have emotionally involving affairs, they can stop thoughts about their lovers, segmenting their inner life, in a way that women seem unable to do.

As we have seen, David's California affair was over for him when he left California. For Annie, cooking a sound and balanced meal in the comfort of her well-furnished middle-class home brought occasional, often unwelcome flashes of her lover's squalid apartment, strewn with dirty clothes and half-eaten cans of poorly nourishing food. Women carry thoughts around with them, imagining their lovers' lives, ruminating about whether or not they have offended or been careful enough with the other's feelings. Women do not turn these thoughts on and off as easily as men do.

"Sometimes the telephone calls would be the worst," Christina recalls. "You go out and make them against all odds. Then you say something that makes you think, 'Oh my God, maybe he took that the wrong way.' But you don't realize that until later, and you can't just call back and make sure that he's okay. So you're stuck thinking about it until the next time you talk to him or until you talk yourself down from the anxiety."

Women seem to be aware, from the beginning, of the impact having an affair might have on their family and friends, as well as on their lovers. Thus, early on, they specify as clearly as possible to their lovers the boundaries around their affairs. This also is a step toward ensuring that these men are not misled. Guilt about being the cause of pain cuts at the heart of their self-respect as women.

Annie explained: "It was very important that Joe understand exactly what the terms were. I didn't want to be left feeling I'd been exploitative at the end. After all, I was the one who was married, with a child, a nice house, and all that." Indeed, women are often disappointed and dismayed by their lovers' failure to be as clear to them about what they can expect. Even when affairs are chiefly about sexual pleasure, women seem to concentrate on others' feelings and by the same token try to safeguard themselves from emotional turmoil. These worries about the potential turmoil and their specification of rules are probably defensive strategies: women know that they must protect themselves from getting too enmeshed with their lovers. The potential difficulty is in maintaining the relationship without getting too close or merging with their partner. For men the difficulty is letting themselves get close enough without the intimacy becoming threatening.

Women and men talk about different things when they discuss their affairs. Men talk about the effects affairs have on their own feelings or on their plans. Women mention how their affairs have affected their children, friends, affair partners, and husbands, as well as themselves. Men do not necessarily mention whether or not someone was hurt. Women are often at pains to tell you that they did all they could to make sure no one was hurt, even if someone was.

Annie's affair with Joe illustrates these features. Her affair was chiefly sexual; its effects were mainly on her sexual confidence and pleasure. Their affair began when her first child was about eight months old.

"It was a revelation. My husband had not been interested in me sexually since the pregnancy, and truthfully, I had pretty much forgotten the idea of myself as sexual as well. Then along comes this incredibly sexy younger man from my evening Italian class—I had decided to get out and do something besides changing diapers for a while—and he starts telling me how he's having fantasies about me. Well, anyway, you can guess what happened. It was absolutely fantastic sexually. But he was not a real competitor for my husband's place, and he knew it. I made it crystal clear to him before anything began that I loved my husband, and being a mother and having a stable family life were central to me. He was a hippy—he thought I was terribly boring and straitlaced—but had this incredible sexual energy. He was fine about the limits; they suited him too. I don't think he would have been interested in me for a moment if I hadn't been married.

"When I was with him—and that would be at his house on certain specified hours of certain days only—I would cook him something nice. I even sometimes washed his socks for him; he was such a slob, I couldn't help it. Sometimes I would think about him alone in his squalid apartment during the week eating cold food out of cans, and I'd feel a little pang. Here I was making great meals for my family, balanced, the seven basic foods and all. But I also knew that this was what suited him. Apart from wanting to be with each other because we had such a great time in bed—and fun out of it too—I felt comforted by the fact that the arrangement suited both of us equally."

Annie met this man at clearly appointed times. There were rules and conventions about what could be mentioned and how far feelings could go. Her family remained resolutely separate from this man. Sex with her husband improved as Annie felt more confident and could fantasize herself in bed with Joe. As long as this suited them both, the affair continued.

When Annie became pregnant again, it dwindled, and her preoccupation with her family and husband increased. To ward off the female tendency to merge, Annie insisted on specifying the boundaries of her affair.

There is another factor at work here. Because of the still extant double standard, women are quicker to feel guilty about being sexual. They are able to see a greater range of possible consequences of affairs because if their affairs are discovered, the dangers are much greater, as we shall see later in this chapter.

In contrast, men report how their affairs have or have not helped them grow psychologically or change, or whether their affairs have made them feel better or worse. They discuss how affairs make them think about their goals: "Do I want to be married? Do I really want this person?" Unlike women, they do not spend much time imagining what their affair partners are really thinking or really wanting, or how to protect their affair partners from making mistaken assumptions about the affair. Unlike women, they assume that these affair partners will themselves find out exactly what the affair means, how far it can go, and how each figures in the other's life and plans.

"Wonderful passion," said Sam of his affair with Ellen. "It made me reevaluate my marriage. It made me think very seriously about whether or not I could leave my marriage for her." David said of his affairs in his open marriage to Ursula, "It makes me feel great—tingly. I love being in love." David also talked about his plans: "I would never leave Ursula, and she [his California lover] obviously did not understand this. Since she wanted more than I did, there was no place for it." Their statements are different: the man's is brief, the woman's more probing.

It is not that men do not care about the impact of their affairs, but they are less aware of the web of effects on others. Similarly, women talk about the effects affairs have on their identity and on their plans, but the subject arises in the context of discussing the web of effects on everyone.

When Linda was struggling to end her two-year love affair with Bill, her suffering was compounded by guilt over the fact that her depression was diverting energy from both her three-year-old daughter and her husband. She was racked with pain over Bill's agony, for he was behaving desperately and demanding that she accommodate his escalating pleas for attention. This was happening just when she was trying to extricate herself from him. She was in a bind. The effect of the affair in the end was a recommitment to her marriage. But in the course of trying to achieve this she also had to look after the very person she was trying to leave.

To be a woman means to consider one's actions within a net-work of social relationships and in relation to others' responses to them. To be a man means to consider one's actions in themselves, how they will project into the future, how one's identity is further shaped or confirmed by them. A net effect of these gender differences is that women are more likely to be emotionally involved in their affairs than men. While women may be having more affairs than they were in the past, their greater emotional involvement makes them likely to have fewer affairs than men. In general, women's affairs, even when clearly limited, demand a greater degree of emotional expenditure than men's.

Model of Marriage and Effects

The expectations one has about marriage in general and one's own in particular obviously affect both the likelihood of an affair and its effects. The marriage-is-for-everything model assumes painful and negative effects; the segmented marriage model believes it is possible to have less overlap between affairs and marriage; in the open model affairs are thought to benefit or else not affect marriages.

In the marriage-is-for-everything model people usually hold that affairs always happen because something is wrong with the marriage. The effects in this kind of marriage are always in some sense bad, even if the couple later acknowledges that an affair has increased their self-esteem, made for better marital relations, or given them valuable knowledge. Affairs are bad because they let a marriage down. Spouses should be able to communicate directly with each other. If either is missing something, it is up to him or her to repair the situation within the relationship. Even if an individual is replenished or a marriage is somehow stabilized by an affair, guilt for failing the marital ideal cancels out the benefits.

A case in point is Simon, a middle-aged chairman of a research institution. He had a brief but intense affair with a much younger woman and briefly thought of ending his marriage. "I looked down the years, and it seemed as if my life might end up like my parents'—domesticity, sameness, people growing to hate each other.

Then along came this delectable girl. She was captivating. She had heard of me and my work, had come to spend time at our institute, especially to be with me. She was in love with me, and at first I felt protective of her. But then, well, it just became harder and harder to resist."

Although he felt revitalized by the affair, he feels he unforgivably betrayed Susie, his wife. Guilt erased the rewards of the affair. But it was through his affair that he realized Susie's cloying dependence on him was draining his desire for her. The jolt his affair gave him stirred him to pressure her to establish her own research project and to move her office to another building. Previously this couple had been inseparable, sharing a home as well as an office. In the aftermath of the affair, their marriage was revitalized. So was Susie's career. Simon, having felt far too merged with Susie for his own comfort, now feels much happier about his marriage. Yet Simon thinks his affair was a terrible mistake: it was a betrayal of the intention and spirit of his marriage. "I will never live down the feeling that I hurt her. I sometimes think about how she looked in those first weeks, and I can hardly bear to live with myself."

In the segmented model the two domains, marriage and affairs, are separate. Yet, even so, people concede indirect effects of affairs. For example, Melissa, a thirty-three-year-old mother of two, reported that although she operated as if her affair and marriage were separate, her affair made her "feel wonderfully sexual," and this had so enlivened her that she was a more cheerful mother and wife.

Laura, as we have seen, claimed that her marriage was much easier as a result of her affairs. It was when she stopped wishing that her husband could be something he was not that she appreciated the qualities he did have. This was possible because she was having great sex and meaningful conversations with her lovers rather than with her husband. But her lovers were not offering her comfortable homes, love for her children, and a stable future. Her husband was.

In the open model, affairs are enhancing as long as they stay within bounds. In this model each member of the couple seeks self-actualization above all else. The model assumes psychological growth. It constrains jealousy and possessiveness, which often get out of control and can be destructive. The ugliness of betrayal is supposedly avoided because there is, first, no secrecy and, second, an understanding it does not constitute betrayal. Ursula's and David's affairs fit this model. David once challenged their contract by getting too attached to his affair partner; that is, from Ursula's perspective he was spending too much time with his lover. More important, he seemed to want to be with her more than with Ursula. The marital contract was challenged. The issue of betrayal arose. Possessiveness and jealousy reared their heads, and mutual confidence was shaken.

Open marriages do not invariably avoid the painful parts of affairs; marital contracts are not always robust, and the temptation to break them can arise. Once that occurs, betrayal becomes the issue, as it did for David and Ursula.

Specific Effects of Affairs

Affairs can bring about personal development, sexual pleasure, changes in marital expectations and satisfaction, and shifts in the quality of friendships. They can also have effects on children.

Both men and women report personal growth through their affairs. In some cases it is through becoming intimate with someone who has stretched their horizons. Ursula, for instance, reported that Sean, an artist, stretched her artistically. Sometimes the affair offers people a completely new experience. Laura learned that she could be sexually abandoned through her affairs: "I'd always felt very sensual, but my husband was embarrassed by it. Since we met when I was about fourteen, I had had no other sexual experience. I remained embarrassed about my feelings until my first affair, and then—pow!—I realized that was his problem, not mine."

Sometimes the affair provides a context in which to reaffirm something one already knew but had lost in oneself. David relearned his romanticism through his affairs.

Sometimes the development is centered on sexuality. This was so in Annie's affair with Joe. Occasionally sexuality is indirectly important. Ursula was at pains to downplay the significance of the sex itself in her affair with Sean. Yet David reported feeling happy for her about her affair because it "does so much for her confi-

dence—and it certainly has made her more uninhibited sexually."
He also reported that he did not feel threatened by Sean since "he
is so completely unlike me. I know that Ursula would never want
him over me. We would never leave each other, as we both have the
ultimate qualities each wants in the other."

Ursula commented in a separate interview, "I am sexually satisfied with David. However, Sean is very sensitive in a way that David
cannot be, and he understands my art—he's an artist—in a way that
David simply could not. More important, though, is the fact that I
have something that's only for me. That makes me feel *so* important, affirmed, desired, and appreciated—and that feeds back into
my sexual relationship with David. Sean just is not as good a lover,
but he adores being with me. We kiss a lot. In some ways it's very
innocent. I just feel romantic, and it's exciting being loved by two
men in very different ways." Her confidence is increased and her
inhibitions are unleashed because "having an affair is illicit. There
were not many things forbidden to me about sex while I was growing
up. But affairs are forbidden. This makes them exciting." So while
sex with Sean is not wildly exciting, Ursula as an adulteress is.

Affairs have brought people increased self-esteem, more sexual
confidence, more insight into how one is with the opposite sex, a
wisdom about relationships, and a greater sense of autonomy.
People sometimes feel that they grew while their marriages suffered.
Yet others report that their own growth took place apart from their
marriages and had no direct effect on them.

There are ample accounts of this kind of impact of affairs, especially in literature and films. An explosion of novels and films of the
late sixties and early seventies focused on women's psychological
growth partly through affairs. *Diary of a Mad Housewife* is emblem-
atic of this. The heroine of the story was jolted enough by her experience of a short and monstrous affair to end her long and dreadful
marriage.

We have fewer stories of men's growth through affairs. Men's
affairs are "macho," "sexual," or "exploitative." Nevertheless, men
do report personal development, their affairs allowing them the
chance to live out different sides of themselves or discover something new. As with women, affairs can give men affirmation. David
said, "It is wonderful to feel as if you are in love again. The chase,

the thrill of new bodies, and the intense desire . . . " Sam's affair with Ellen, in addition to the sex, made him feel understood: "We were just so simpatico. She was the girl my mother wished I had married. She really knew me, understood where I was coming from. The feelings were very powerful."

There are two major gender differences, however: First, more men than women describe affairs as "just sexual." This difference may be in part a linguistic one, but it underscores the different sexual approaches of men and women. "Just sexual" is acceptable language for men. Women have different ways of saying it—such as sex in the affair was the "main point of interest" or satisfaction. This is usually followed up by "it was not just sex." This difference is not surprising, given that women are likely to be more emotionally connected in any case. For example, in Annie's first affair, Joe's desire for her was the main attraction. However, Annie quickly pointed out that she liked Joe and he liked her, that she thought about him and his welfare from time to time in between seeing him, and that she cared about the effects of their affair on him. She even performed "wifely" duties—such as cooking and washing his socks for him.

Second, women more often than men describe the consequences for others of their own personal development. For example, Melissa reported that her affair made her feel "sexy again after all those years of being primarily a mother—and mothers just aren't sexy. That was great—a real revelation for me. Just what I needed at that time. It was great fun. Because I felt so great I was a much better mother and wife during it and afterward, too." This is in contrast to Sam: "I have had lots of affairs. I travel a lot. It probably has to do with the fact that I was not very confident in school—my family moved every few years and I never felt accepted in any school. I wasn't a particularly good athlete and I was smaller than most of the other boys since I was younger. So in a way I'm making up for lost time. I want to be able to feel that if I feel sexual with someone it is possible to have an affair." Affairs are conduits to feeling for him and connections he makes with women. In contrast to Melissa, Sam does not mention the effects on his wife—good or bad. As we have said, men are not as conscious of the web of effects, as they assume less responsibility for the feelings of others. Therefore, their own self-growth is seen more clearly in isolation from its effects on others. We are talking here about general, group differences or tendencies for men and women. Reports do seem to differ by gender, particularly when men or women are not consumed by guilt.

It should be pointed out here, though, that many men feel terribly guilty about having had affairs. These are often men, such as Simon, whose marriages are in the marriage-is-for-everything model. But their guilt about having betrayed their marriages apparently cancels benefits of any sort. The model also means a preoccupation with the effects of an affair on one's spouse, and by implication, a concern about the effects on the affair partner. Since you are supposed to be fully committed to your marriage you have by definition led someone else astray.

Affairs can also produce reconsideration of the purpose of marriage; through affairs, a redefinition of marriage can evolve; and there may also be a reevaluation of what is possible and desirable in your own marriage. There can be any of these possible consequences: an affirmation that everything is fine as it is; a conclusion that something critical is missing in your marriage and it is dead without it; a decision to accept the limitations of your marriage and an acceptance of affairs as compensatory; or a commitment to try to move the marriage closer to your ideal.

Men and women differ in another respect. Women are likely to report more subtle effects of their relationships. Indeed, they seem to look for effects. Again, this is consistent with their socialization. Women have the language for describing both the feelings and the effects of those feelings on others. That is why Melissa said that if she felt better, that would affect her marriage, while Sam did not.

Even if they can separate their affairs from their marriages, most women will discover connections in indirect ways, as Melissa did. Susannah, who is forty-eight, had four affairs which she termed serious in twenty-three years of marriage. From a wealthy and privileged background, in which both parents had affairs when she was growing up, Susannah owns her own interior design business. Her husband is often away on business, and her friendships with both men and women occupy much of her time and energy. She felt "something like love" in each of her affairs. In two she had long-standing friendships with her partners, both before and after the affair. Yet her feelings for her husband remain unchanged. She loves him above all.

The spinoff for Susannah's marriage has been an increased freedom and a focus on its strengths rather than on what she lacks. She and her husband still have a sexual life, but it is not the main point of their joint life. Sex is infrequent and warm but not exciting. She has reevaluated and redefined her marriage. "Why should Paul have to be everything for me? He is a terrific, dynamic man, a great provider. We share a sense of humor, tastes, and a long history. I have never met a man I respect so much and find overall so interesting and attractive. We now have a relationship that works in most ways except his ability to give me time and attention and to be demonstrative. That's as much my problem as his. I solve it by not straining to fit him into the box I need but to look elsewhere for that. I think our marriage works."

Both men and women say that affairs have revealed things they want to change in their marriages. But in trying to enact changes, results have varied. For example, Nick, an academic, realized that he needed more affection, more sexual experimentation, and more talking with his wife. She was accommodating about more sexual experimentation, but she is a cool and distant woman for whom talking and demonstrativeness do not come easily. The marriage improved only slightly in those respects.

As a result of her passionate affair with Bill, Linda lobbied for more intimacy with her husband, Peter. She was more successful. Six years after her affair with Bill ended, the couple is closer and happier than ever before. "I still have to do a lot more of the prodding to get things out into the open, but it's much better. Sex is good, as it had been once before. We're really close and warm, and we are really a good, happy and close family. We've moved on. We really have."

Finally, sometimes an affair illustrates so much that is wrong with a marriage that it ends. Kate and Jonathan have now been married for fifteen years. Their affair crystallized the feeling they both had that their respective marriages were already dead.

Affairs can also ring changes in the network of other relationships, outside of the immediate family and the affair partner. People in secret affairs often look for trusted, safe confidants, but they may find them in unlikely places. Or secrecy can breed silence and change the nature of formerly intimate friendships, sometimes leading to isolation. Almost all of Linda's spare time was spent with Bill, although she was characteristically very gregarious. Moreover, she suspected that her closest friends, to whom she might have confided her affair, would be judgmental because Bill was professionally involved with Peter, her husband. This led to silence and further isolation.

In secret affairs both men and women often feel a pressure to confide, especially if an affair brings on new or confusing feelings. For example, Sam, feeling unbalanced by the torrent of emotions unleashed in his affair, deliberately confided in someone safely distant. Laura, who told Emily about one of her affairs, discovered that Emily also had affairs. The double secrecy bound them together and intensified their friendship.

People have commented, "I really knew who my friends were during that time." The configuration of friendships is often profoundly affected by an affair: certain people with whom one might have been very close cannot be told and are avoided, while others who can be told move into the inner circle.

Having an affair can also affect the network of relationships because the need for secrecy can be isolating. "I wish I could have told people. Having the affair really cut me off from my friends and made me lonely," Linda said after her affair ended. And, as she experienced, that very isolation can intensify the affair and make the affair partner even more special, important, and needed.

This can happen to both men and women, but the reasons it happens differ. Men, who find it easier to confide in women, may discover that the affair partner is the only person in whom they can confide because of the secrecy. She becomes the woman in whom they confide about feelings the affair itself stirs up. For women, the secrecy takes on an increased urgency: they need not only to protect their marriages but to safeguard their reputations. This may drive a woman more profoundly into the affair, the only place she can talk about feelings aroused by it. And because there is always a tendency for women to become too involved, too merged, the isolation that breeds further dependence on the affair can reinforce this tendency.

Since women are more accustomed to talking about their feelings, they usually find someone in whom to confide. But their guilt about an affair may be compounded because they are concealing important feelings from their women friends, denying them the usual currency of female friendship. Again, this is consistent with the gender divide: women tend to confide in a wider network of people, including their women friends. If those avenues for confiding are cut off, as in Linda's case, they endure deep isolation. For many men this isolation is not foreign. They would not have confided in friends in any case, and isolation would not have driven them to cast their social net more widely in an attempt to find a safe confidant.

For many women isolation intensifies the need to confide. Either the woman then turns to the affair partner, increasing his significance and centrality, or she looks for another (usually female) confidante, running the risk of rejection or, worse, discovery or betrayal. Alternatively, she waits out the isolation, with varying consequences. It should be noted that many people do not have the choice—they cannot confide in others. There may be no safe or suitable person in whom to confide. The person having the affair may choose to be isolated rather than to confide or may have no choice but to be isolated. This Hobson's choice may be one reason many people turn at this point to therapists. They are presumed to be safe confidants.

One consequence of this isolation can be depression, particularly over one's marriage. Diana went on a two-week vacation to a tennis camp—her first gesture of independence in ten years. She was then thirty years old. She had been engaged at eighteen, married at twenty, and her first child was on the way at twenty-one. Throughout her marriage Diana had been her husband's assistant, running the office of his architectural practice. After her youngest child went off to school, she began to feel increasingly lethargic and discontented. When a friend asked her to accompany her to a tennis camp, Diana somewhat apathetically thought it "might be a good idea." Her husband, annoyed by her listlessness, encouraged her to go. There she had an affair with her instructor. Although Diana thought of it at the time as "only a fling" and did not expect to see the man again, after she returned home her depression deepened. She could not confide in her husband about the source of her depression, nor did she want to risk telling anyone else. (Her friend who had accompanied her to the camp did not know about the affair.) Her isolation increased her depression, and for many months her marriage was in a painful state.

A strategy for dealing with the isolation that an affair brings is to decrease the preoccupation with it. Men, being better at cutting off, are more successful at managing this than women. When women try to limit their affairs from the start by specifying rules to their lovers, they are also trying to tell themselves not to let the affair spill over into the rest of their lives. They are trying to prevent thoughts and longings from taking over. Although women are increasingly able to compartmentalize by specifying and keeping to boundaries, men are better at it. The following illustrates how neatly men can cut off or segment.

Nick has a regular business meeting in a foreign country once a year. After he had ended an intense, marriage-threatening affair that his wife discovered, their marriage eventually became an open one. This was because, after trying monogamy again for a while, he convinced his wife that forbidding affairs would endanger their marriage. He resented her for what felt to him like her control over him, and this imperiled their marriage. She agreed, in principle, to try an open marriage model this time, and they forged a new marital contract. Soon afterward she had to adjust to the contract in practice when Nick confessed that he had been having an ongoing affair with Ghisela, a Belgian who attends the yearly meeting. They sleep together only at this time. Ghisela is also married. During this week-long meeting they sleep together, as they have been doing for the past ten years.

Because this affair fits the new marital contract Nick and his wife have worked out, which allows Nick to have affairs with other women as long as they do not threaten the survival or primacy of his marriage, his wife has discovered that she can tolerate this affair; it is compartmentalized in time, space, and emotional content. Nick assumes that this affair will continue indefinitely. He does not think much about Ghisela when they are apart, but he does look forward to their yearly reunion. We do not know whether Ghisela is as blasé as Nick, although Nick's wife suspects that she is not; she reports that there are phone calls and letters between meetings. Nick denies communicating himself.

Another consequence of isolation attendant upon an affair can be increased self-reliance. Particularly for women, having something that they manage on their own can feel like a real achievement. Christina's first affair was an example of this; it revealed her effectiveness. Partly through it she pushed back the limited frontiers of her life, which had come to be lived very much within her own four walls. She had been crippled by a dance injury and was very much stuck in the house looking after small children. After a successful operation that freed her movement, she began to work her way back slowly into the dance world; in doing so, she began to commute to London one day a week, sometimes staying overnight for a second. Simultaneously, both her children were then in full-time school and her husband, who had changed jobs, was able to look after the children. The headiness of her expanding life made her particularly susceptible to the attentions of a former colleague, and they began an affair. Among other things, the actual management of the affair, demanding time and attention away from her family as well as canny and cool management of the secrecy, taught her that she was much more organized and in control than she had formerly imagined.

There are effects on the affair partner as well as effects on the marriage. When secret affairs are discovered, the impact on affair partners is often similar to that on the spouses: jealousy, anger, and possessiveness run riot. A sense of betrayal, perhaps for choosing the spouses or expressing divided loyalties, is also aroused. And guilt for being in an affair often rises keenly at this point if it has not been around all along. Jessica spent a lot of time feeling guilty about her affair with Daniel, in part because she considered herself a feminist. "How can I be a good feminist, a 'sister' to Daniel's wife, if I am having an affair with her husband?" She felt less guilty when the affair came to light than she did before. She felt betrayed by Daniel, who suddenly felt bound by loyalty to his wife when she showed how hurt and angry he had made her.

There is another side to the coin. Affair partners, particularly in long-term affairs, think that they are the chosen, loved, special ones. (Sometimes there is some justification for this, but not always.) Lovers stick with wives and husbands out of habit, duty, history, and because of the children. But love, sex, attraction, and excitement draw the lover to the affair partner. When Daniel's wife found out about Jessica and Daniel's affair, at first he promised Jessica he would live with her, but then he went back to his wife. At that point he wrote to Jessica, saying he would always love her, would love no one as he had her, but he "could not do this" to his children. He was not sure his wife could cope. He did not see how he could throw away all those years of marriage; that would not have been fair to his wife. Moreover, his parents deeply disapproved of his leaving his family. Jessica was heartbroken, of course, and as of her last interview with us, she is still waiting for him to change his mind, waiting for the strength of their love to triumph over the dullness of his familial duty.

In other cases habit and obligation support the continuance of the affair, just as they are supposed to support the continuance of the marriage. Sharon continued to see her lover, who worked on the support staff in her office, partly because she felt she owed it to him. He expected to see her and to sleep with her, and she did not want to hurt him or let him down. Being concerned about his feelings went a long way toward sustaining their affair.

Frequently the affair partner stays because he or she thinks the affair will turn into a marriage. Nora, who was unmarried, met Max, her first serious lover, when she was twenty-three. He was thirty-five, married, with two children. They met regularly two nights a week for ten years, and in the summer they spent most of one month together while his family stayed at their summer home in the country and he worked in the city during the week.

Nora truly believed Max would leave his wife and marry her when his children were old enough. She was prepared to wait. But after ten years she wanted children; she began pressing him to divorce his wife. Max made vague promises, but nothing changed and Nora grew increasingly resentful. Max's children were preparing to leave home, but Max showed no signs of doing so himself. One day Nora met Max's wife in the elevator at his office. Tempted to confront her, she resisted the urge. But she was sure that Max's wife knew who she was; something in her stare convinced her. Shortly afterward his wife somehow discovered the affair—Nora thinks that seeing her made certain suspicions click and with a little detective work the affair was uncovered. Although Nora thought this would surely be her chance, it worked out quite differently. Max broke off with her. As in many stories of the "other woman," Nora lost every-thing. After ten years, she is now in her thirties, wants children badly, and is out dating again, this time alone and bitter.

Some people do marry their affair partners. Kate and Jonathan married and have stayed happily married for fifteen years. In chap-ter 8 we will see that while in some cases affairs do go on to become marriages, in others affairs cannot manage the transition. In still others, like Nora and Max's, the affairs never even get to the first stage of the transition from affair to marriage.

Other affair partners remain in affairs, maintaining the new sta-tus quo, because the limits of affairs suit them. This is especially true if they, too, are married. Marie, a fifty-one-year-old psycholo-gist, has had six affairs while married. In one she fell in love with someone who lived in a different country. The tendency to merge, the compulsion to think and talk about her affair partner, to guess his thoughts, and to wonder obsessively whether or not she was cen-tral to his, began to overtake her, disturbing her stability. For this reason she preferred, on balance, that her lover live far away rather than near, although she was unhappy about that as well. The fact that he, too, was married was both maddening—it made her jealous and prevented access to him even further—and also comforting, because it helped preserve her own marriage.

As we have already mentioned, most women automatically men-tion effects on their affair partners when discussing their affairs. Witness Susannah, the forty-eight-year-old interior designer men-tioned earlier: "I did feel I loved Colin in a way, and I let him know in what way: he was so much fun, and we had a great time in bed. I made sure that he knew this, but also that Paul was number one. It was always very clear *when* I could be available for Colin and for *what*, and that I would make myself available then and only then. I often would think of him on his own or with his wife, whom he loved in his way, too, though they had a dreadful sex life. I knew he was okay, and that made me feel all right going off with Paul. I knew Colin was fine without me. I always made sure I understood what Colin wanted from me, and when it looked as if he might want more, I started to cool it. I was not going to hurt him if at all possi-ble. We finally ended it when Colin met someone who wanted him more than I did, and he felt ready to leave his wife. This other woman was ready and waiting for him in a way I would never be. We're still good friends, and there are absolutely no hard feelings. On the contrary, I think we both feel we gave each other a lot and were very straight and fair with each other."

While men manage to conduct their affairs without much thought to the effects on their partners, they may well face them in its aftermath. David reported being surprised at first by the vitriolic reaction of his California lover. From her point of view she had been dumped. From his, the end of the trip meant the end of the escapade. "She knew I was married, didn't she?" he said. David's affairs can be very passionate, he said. Boxed off as they are by the rules of his open marriage, they are removed from the day-to-day reality of his life, conducted as if in a hothouse and with the knowledge that when the intensity dies, so will the affair. These rules prevent him from becoming involved over any length of time. The affairs, in turn, because they can be intense, if brief and limited, protect him from becoming too close to Ursula, his wife. In his lover's eyes it may have been David's responsibility to spell out more than "I'm married," but David saw things differently. David said he told her "that I have an open marriage, that Ursula is the most important person in the world to me. No one challenges that." If the woman went ahead and read between the lines, interpreted as she liked—perhaps thinking that no one ever really knows where new emotions will take them and that maybe David's experience with her would be so momentous he would have to carry on with her despite his marital rules—that was her business, as far as David was concerned. If she misread things, that was her mistake, and she has to live with the consequences rather than try to foist them onto him. If she needed clearer facts, she should have gotten them. Men act; if they need facts, they get them. They do not expect someone else to lead them there.

While Sam had had brief affairs during his eight-year marriage, the one with Ellen was different. He seriously contemplated leaving his wife for her. Ellen's marriage was faltering when they began to see each other, and she pressed him for a decision. Ellen had been supportive during the terrible time his parents were ill. When they finally died, within a year of each other, Sam felt at loose ends, while Ellen's marriage at the time was practically over. Sam equivo-

cated about leaving his wife, and Ellen grew bitter. At first her bitterness baffled him: where was the supportive, understanding
woman he had come to love? Nursing his pain for a long time, he
gradually accepted Ellen's rejection. Unfortunately for Ellen, Sam
had a different view of marriage. "Look," he explained, "my marriage is not bad, just limited. I am bound to Marlene by our history,
her affection, and my appreciation of her calmness and acceptance.
We never fight. We get along day-to-day in a very amiable way. I
know that's not the sort of life I would have had with Ellen. It
would have been from one fraught moment to another. We would
have fought. Everything became a fight. She can't relax. It wasn't so
simple for me, as if 'I have a bad marriage, so I'd better leave it for
you.'" When his grief and mourning began to abate, he grew more
sure, rather than less, that he needed his serene and accepting wife.
Years later he thinks of Ellen and sees more clearly how she must
have felt—her marriage was not as comfortable as his—and he
regrets her pain.

Another example of the peculiarly male ability to cut off from
the lover's perspective is John, who fell in love with his affair partner and intended to marry her. But John is a devout Catholic whose
faith in the end short-circuited his affair. Twenty-eight-years-old, a
teacher, he was married for five years to a woman he has known
since childhood. He met Caroline, a fellow teacher, in a counseling
course. Caroline was divorced and at the end of an affair "going
nowhere." She was substantially older and more worldly than John,
and he saw her as a woman with a strong spiritual side who had
been badly treated by the men in her life.

Caroline and John were passionate as he had never been with his
wife, whom he had married primarily out of a sense of responsibility.
He and Caroline talked abut marriage from the beginning, and he
was acutely aware of her need for a stable relationship. But when
the time came, the reality of leaving his wife seemed impossible;
more important, if he left her, he did not see how he could continue
in his faith. He did an about-face, rejecting Caroline completely. He
refused to see her or contact her. Although he assured her that he
could recognize how deeply painful his decision was for her, he also
communicated his dismay that the impossibility of their relationship was not so manifest to her—as such a deeply spiritual

woman—as it had become to him. In the end Caroline was more horribly betrayed than ever; John was supposed to have been different. But John made his decision without reference to Caroline; to do so he had to cut off from his feelings for her and erase thoughts of her reaction.

Months after the affair was over, when he could consider his feelings from a distance, they met again. At that point her sorrow was more poignant and naked to him. By then he had lived with his decision, become more comfortable with it, and he could afford to become less defensive and empathically take her perspective. Earlier, in order to act, he had had to blind himself to it.

Cause and Effect and Back Again: The Synergy Between Marriage and Affairs

Quite apart from these specific effects there is also a synergistic relationship between affairs and marriage, both cause and effect at the same time. People live in marriages and affairs simultaneously. For some people living in each is like existing in two separate narratives. Christina's first affair was mostly like that, cut off in both time and place more or less regularly as it was. Nick's affair with Ghisela is another example of this. But these separate narratives reflect on each other.

Christina's sex with her lover reflected the segmentation in her marriage; her children and domestic life reflected what was missing from her affair. But for others, having an extramarital affair is like living in one narrative in which events from one inform events from the other. The quality of each is affected by the other and help give each their meaning. For instance, coming back feeling wonderful about one's lover may deflate one's feelings about one's spouse. This was certainly true for Linda, who grew more and more distant, disenchanted, and angry with Peter as she grew more involved with Bill. Or, as Melissa experienced, it can enhance one's feelings about one's spouse and domestic life. Feeling good in one can help make one feel good in the other.

The influence of marriage on affair and vice versa can also lead to the breakup of either the marriage or the affair. Demands from Ellen on Sam to divorce his wife made him end his affair with Ellen. Sexual excitement and intimacy with Daniel led Jessica to acquiesce in her husband's wish to separate.

Some people who have had affairs see marriage as a membrane. It can change form and shape, sometimes incorporating affairs and becoming different in character while the affair exists, then changing again when it is over. They learn something profound about marriage: that it changes in quality as other events, such as deaths, births, job changes, moves, and also, it seems, affairs, affect it. People can no longer subscribe to the static, romanticized notion of marriage with which they began. But they often have a more profound respect for it as an institution as they watch it adapt.

A large number of affairs do not wreck lives or marriages, but certainly some do. The relationship between affairs and divorce is often assumed to be stronger than it probably is. In chapter 8 we will examine this relationship more fully.

The Impact on Children of Affairs

The common line about affairs is that they must affect children adversely. But if an affair is kept secret and separate and if people do manage to segment affairs and marriage, cutting off when they are not with their affair partners, why should children be affected? In segmented marriages in which the affair is successfully kept secret, children may not be affected, just as spouses may not. Melissa reported an indirect benefit from her affair to her children: "I felt better about myself, therefore I was more cheerful, and therefore I was a more cheerful, resilient mother." It is not necessarily the affair, per se, but its damaging impact on the parent or threatening effects on the marriage that affect children.

There is the obvious point that children are upset by marital disharmony, by fighting, by seeing their parents depressed or unhappy with each other, and by the lack of energy parents have for them when they are depressed or else preoccupied with the potential breakdown of their marriage. Sometimes children do not like to be around the affair partner even if they do not know that an affair is going on. This happens in cases in which they ascertain, either by witnessing some striking show of emotion or by the affair partner taking up too much of the parent's time or performing the other parent's functions, that someone is having an effect on their parent that rivals or detracts from the other parent (or themselves). Children resent people of the opposite sex making that parent too happy or taking them away from their other parent.

An example is that of Alexandra, an eight-year-old who lives with her mother now that her parents' marriage has ended. Alexandra has never been told the true story of her parentage nor of the reasons for her parents' marital breakup. While her parents were married, her mother began an affair with her boss and became pregnant. Unable to have an abortion because of religious convictions, she confessed her affair to her husband. He agreed to accept the baby as his own if she would agree to leave her job and end the affair. When Alexandra was four, her mother returned to work part-time. Her work as a systems analyst brought her into renewed contact with her old lover, whom she began to see again, sometimes at home, since he expressed interest and curiosity in seeing Alexandra, his biological daughter. When her husband found out about the renewed affair, he left her, although he still recognized Alexandra as his own daughter and made arrangements for joint custody after the divorce.

Alexandra has never liked her mother's lover, even though she has been told nothing of this story but only that "Daddy and Mommy stopped loving each other and could not get along together anymore." When her biological father comes into the room, Alexandra says that she feels uncomfortable and changes seats if seated near him.

Such discomfort sometimes develops when the climate at home changes. For example, Michele's ten-year-old son, Ethan, got along very well with her research colleague, Tom, whom he had known as long as he could remember because his mother had always worked closely with him. Tom used to take him to sports events with his daughters. Michele's husband, Paul, was often away and was not much interested in sports anyway. When Michele and Paul began to have marital problems, which coincided with the breakup of Tom's marriage, Ethan began to act decidedly cool toward Tom and, moreover, became surly and difficult with his mother. This surliness was aggravated whenever Ethan suspected that Michele had spent time with Tom. Ethan felt threatened by Tom, who had begun to have an affair with her soon after his wife left him.

Ethan was correctly sensing the shift in their relationship and the attendant one in his parents'—as well as the potential threat to that relationship. Michele was racked by difficult decisions at that point: "When I started to have my affair with Tom, I just knew it was going to be over with Paul; I just could not go near him sexually. I talk with Tom about everything. We feed each other intellectually. Paul and I don't have that and never did." Clearly, her affair with Tom made her feel discontented with both intimacy and sex in her marriage. Her relationship with Paul became more distant and discordant. Ethan noticed this and also noticed that his mother was cheerful when she was with Tom and was spending more time with him.

These children are acting similarly to children of divorced or separated parents, often resenting the new partner for stepping into the other parent's place. Children also can feel during parental affairs that they are in the middle. Adolescents are particularly vulnerable to this triangulation. Because adolescents are adultlike in many respects, parents needing support may, inappropriately, lean on them. When Karen's father was having an affair with his secretary, he confided in her about the affair and his intention to leave her mother when the "time was right." Loyal to her father and afraid of upsetting her mother, Karen kept this secret.

In the meantime her mother suffered from myriad psychosomatic complaints, and the marriage, never good, further deteriorated. Karen withdrew from both parents, and her schoolwork began to suffer. A year later her father told her that he had had a child with the other woman. Ultimately Karen left home, angry at her father, and also at her mother for not standing up to him.

Sally's mother drew her daughters around her like a blanket when her husband went off to France with another woman. He was "shiftless," "irresponsible," a "hopeless romantic," while she was blameless, a model wife, treated badly by her fool of a husband. Her daughters, who had formerly adored him, for he was fun-loving, affectionate, and warm with them (entirely unlike their mother), began to view him with contempt. This was especially so when he returned a short time later, minus the other woman, begging to be taken back. Even now, thirty years later, his daughters side with their mother in the firm belief that he was "shiftless," "irresponsible," a "hopeless romantic," with their mother his poor victim. The daughters' loyalty to both parents was challenged, and they lost one parent as a result. In Karen's case, she lost both.

Obviously, when a secret affair is discovered, a stage when a marriage may become deeply unstable, children are affected by the turmoil. When Richard's affair was discovered, Polly told their two children. They supported her and went against Richard at first. Then, feeling left out by both parents as they fought each other bitterly, they began to act out, getting into minor scrapes and failing in school.

The effects on children of marriages in turmoil because of affairs varies with a child's age. Younger children will be affected in obvious ways by overt marital dysfunction. Their needs for time and attention are great, and these may be subverted by their parents' marital dramas. Older or adolescent children, who are more independent, will be affected in more subtle ways; their trust and belief in stable partnerships might be shaken, or their need for refuge in a relationship of their own creation might be forged at that point. Moreover, adolescent children are probably more attuned to their parents' sexual relationship and to whether there are sexual undercurrents in their parents' other relationships. In addition, since they may also act as confidants to their parents, given their age, they may be explicitly drawn into their parents' marital dramas and affairs.

Even adult children are affected by their parents having affairs. Adult children are more likely to know about affairs because they are more likely to notice or be told by their parents. Dennis was extremely upset when his mother left his father after forty-two years of marriage; she was "fed up with his other women." Dennis never knew that his father, a well-known playwright, had been unfaithful. Now, forced to think about it, he realized that it was entirely possible the friendships his parents had formed over the years with certain actresses and agents, and one journalist in particular, were probably not as innocent as he had thought. These had been his father's girlfriends, and his mother had known. He felt angry at both his parents; he felt they had deceived and duped him into believing they had one kind of marriage when in fact they had had a different kind altogether. One of his siblings sided with his father, while he felt more sympathetic toward his mother. So even his relationship with his siblings became strained by their respective anger and pain.

Yet some people recount being unaffected by their parents' open affairs. Ted knew of his father's open affair with Camilla, a younger unmarried neighbor. His mother accepted it. His father's loyalty to the family was unquestioned. Eventually the affair ended when the family moved away, and he thinks that Camilla finally married. It may be significant, however, that in Ted's family history affairs had been common for several generations. Fidelity, it seems, was a peripheral value: sharing tastes, background, and experiences, enjoying each other's company, and stable family life were far more central themes.

Other adult children report having had to take sides: "It was selfish of him to do that—it must have hurt her," was the way Michael talked of his memory of his father's "flings," as he called them. Whether these grown-up children have affairs in their own marriages is influenced by this history—or their family scripts, as psychiatrist and family therapist John Byng-Hall calls them. But each script may call for different denouements. Susannah, the child of a home in which affairs were openly tolerated, carries on "discreet" affairs. Her model of marriage is very like that of her parents, which survived over fifty years. Michael's feelings are more ambivalent. He has affairs and feels bad about them. For him secrecy is particularly important if there are children in a marriage. Memories of having to comfort his mother when his father ran off with the nanny haunt him still.

Retrospective accounts such as these may be rewriting history, but we can speculate that children can feel confused by knowing about a parent's liaison with someone who is not their other parent. Certainly, if the child is forced to side with one parent over the other, as Michael was, affairs are going to be painful. On the other hand, if a child feels that the family is secure, perhaps he or she can accept parental affairs with equanimity, as Susannah and Ted report they did.

Emotional Involvement and the Impact of Affairs

The impact of an affair also depends on how strongly people feel about their affair partners. Christina's two affairs show this. When she was first interviewed for this book, she was having an affair that barely affected her marriage. She adored her affair partner, but she loved her husband. A few years later, after that affair had ended relatively painlessly, she fell in love with her husband's best friend. Consumed by her feelings for him, she could barely focus on her husband. Even before she disastrously told him, her marriage had deteriorated under the impact of her passion for her lover.

Limited emotional involvement often means limited impact on the marriage, as Christina's first affair demonstrated. Perhaps she could have gone on having affairs if all had remained limited. But, as we mentioned in our discussion of risks in affairs, one risk is that people cannot always be sure that their feelings will remain in neat compartments, as Christina found out in her second affair.

Discovering a Secret Affair

The impact of discovering a secret affair, whether it is revealed through exposure or through a spouse's disclosure, is of a different order altogether. Any good effects up to that point can be vitiated. The impact of discovering that vows were broken, evidence was hidden, lies were told, and other deceits were committed is traumatic to any partnership, let alone a marriage, which is supposed to be built on honesty. It explicitly demands monogamy. Unless a marriage is open, its foundation of trust and its rules have been violated.

When a secret affair comes to light, no matter whether the impulse to tell has come from a desire to make the marriage better, at one end of a continuum, or to end it, at the other, a period of increased bad feeling ensues. This is more so if the affair has been exposed rather than disclosed. The spouse feels betrayed. The betrayed spouse, feeling fully justified as victim, heaps pain and anger on the betrayer. But if the affair has ended, the spouse who had the affair is often grieving for its loss. If it is continuing, he or she feels caught in the middle. Resentment of the spouse's pressuring can even precipitate a turning away from the spouse and toward the affair partner.

Even when an affair is revealed long after it has ended, the spouse who had the affair usually remembers feeling, or even continues to feel, some attachment to the affair partner. There will often be something good to be remembered or cherished. The opposing positions in which spouses find themselves tend to become entrenched, exaggerated, distorted, and deeply polarized.

"She could only talk about what a shit this girl was, what a moral degenerate. How stupid and hollow she must have been to try to take someone else's husband away right from under her nose," recalled Simon. "It was very painful because I couldn't say, 'No, no. It's not like that! She's adorable. She's young. She was in love, and people believe that love is a justification for all sorts of things. She didn't deliberately set out to hurt you. She's not a bitch—far from it!' But if I were to say anything like that, it would be like poking Susie in the heart with a poisoned arrow. So I had to just bear it. I wanted to kill her at times. Hearing that abuse was part of the worst of it."

Pain divides rather than unites when a partner is the cause of it. Susie recalled the worst of the time following the discovery of Simon's affair: "I didn't want him to touch me for the longest time. Those red lips. I kept thinking of them and how he had kissed them and then . . . I definitely wanted to stay far away from him."

Guilt drives the spouse defensively further away from the other. When this process begins, when pain and guilt are heavy between them, the couple enters a phase that Emily Brown has called obsession with the affair. It is a deeply divisive stage. Yet the mutual obsession joins the couple. They are stuck, with the affair still dividing them and yet without the resolution of either divorce or recon-

ciliation. For the injured spouse the obsession includes a preoccupation with the affair partner and the details of the affair, which feels
both perverse and gripping: Is he/she better than I? Does this mean
that my spouse is less than or more than a man/woman than I
thought? What has my marriage meant? What have I meant to
him/her? How could I have trusted him/her? How can I continue to
do so? What else have I been betrayed about? What else do I not
know about him/her? The marriage feels like a house of cards.

For the spouse who has had the affair, it sometimes means
defending the affair partner. This slows the ending of feelings for
him or her and also drives another wedge between the couple. In
this phase the spouse who had the affair often undergoes terrible
self-doubt, feeling cruel and vile for inflicting such pain. This is so
even when affairs have been valuable and important. Others can get
caught up in the affair at this stage, too. For in this phase sides can
get taken, children can become triangulated, and friendships can be
severed.

Some couples never progress beyond this phase—the marriage is
stuck in a quagmire, doomed to its pain. It is very difficult to move
beyond it. Paradoxically, it seems, in trying to leave the affair, couples can get stuck in its aftermath for the rest of their married life.
In some cases this aftermath is what ends marriages, rather than the
affair itself. Thus, the impulse to confess, even though it may come
from noble intentions and benign motivations, such as to relieve
guilt or clear the air, may backfire. Revelation of a formerly secret
affair leads to the most painful stage of the affair for the marriage.

This is not to say that disclosure in itself is always destructive. It
can be the catalyst for rebuilding, even strengthening, a marriage.
But this depends in part on what model of marriage both partners
desire. If one spouse wants to continue the segmented model with
its attendant secrecy or to move to an open marriage while the
other wants to return to marriage-is-for-everything, rebuilding is
doomed. It also depends on whether in the aftermath of disclosure
both spouses learn something from the affair, detach from it, and
focus instead on new goals for their marriage.

A marriage undergoes other traumas in the aftermath of discovery. When an affair is discovered it usually becomes public. The
spouse who discovers often confides in others. This can also mean

that the one who is having or had the affair turns to outsiders, who may not be impartial and reinforce one side against the other. Sides are taken and battle lines are drawn. Friendships change and are sometimes broken. Loyalties thicken and may not shift even if the couple puts the affair behind them.

When the newly unemployed Matthew left his wife and children to go around the world with his lover, his wife, Elizabeth, in her shock and distress confided in many people, including her elderly mother. She knows that her mother could never contemplate forgiving him. To have taken Matthew back would have entailed a breach with her mother. "She would never understand if I took him back," Elizabeth explained. "She'd think I was a gutless fool." The couple eventually divorced, but at one point, when Matthew's affair had ended and he had found a job in another city, he stayed at the family home while he visited their children on weekends. For a brief period he and Elizabeth slept together, but then he started to see his old lover again. She kept this secret from their children (he went to the guest bed before dawn). She also refrained from telling her friends and, of course, her mother. After casting herself as the hapless victim of the cruelty of a moral reprobate, she could not very well justify sleeping with the enemy.

If the publicity or uproar surrounds children, things grow even more complicated. Valerie and Julian's eight- and eleven-year-old daughters felt like parcels bouncing back and forth between parents and various friends who had taken sides. Julian became very depressed on discovering Valerie's affair, while Valerie responded with self-righteous indignation, blaming him for driving her to it through his passivity and sexual indifference. From one day to the next they made plans to separate, first with Julian leaving, then Valerie. Each time they told the girls. Each time they changed their minds. The couple eventually tried reconciliation, taking a family vacation. Before long the two girls were avoiding going home, turning up on neighbors' doorsteps at dinnertime, looking sad and bewildered.

Valerie and Julian's daughters did not takes sides, but Richard and Polly's children did. Both children were openly contemptuous of their father. His constant apologies reminded them of his transgression and renewed their mother's pain. They said, "Anyone who has an affair is dirt." Anger at the affair also permits other, older anger to surface: Why was he so marginal? Why didn't he care enough about them to take time with them when they were little? Together, mother and children continued to marginalize him through their contempt.

There is also lasting, if diminished pain when marriages successfully survive the post-discovery phase. Susie will never forget her shock and insecurity. "It is like the death of a loved one: it lives in my memory, like a scar," she said. It is a sadness she has buried but that she will not forget. It is possible to spark her pain, although it may be harder these days than earlier. Moreover, the model of their marriage is now fixed, rigid: no affair jokes are allowed. Rules are set. Marriages that have endured discovery and survived, that are mended, are usually marriages where the couple feels they must stick to rules.

Discovery can yield a real or an important change in a marriage, or it can consign it to terrible pain and even break it apart. In any case, it should be remembered that no matter what the outcome, it produces a difficult, unsettled, and painful aftermath that cannot be avoided. Sometimes it takes a dose of something from outside— most commonly marital counseling or therapy—as an antidote to the pain, as we will discuss later in this chapter. And it should also be remembered that despite everyone's best efforts, the risk in secret affairs is that they will be discovered, although many do remain secret.

Guilt and Disclosure: The Desire to Tell

Some people disclose because of guilt. The guilt may arise from the fact that they are withholding something from the marriage that has been promised to or is acknowledged to belong to the spouse, or it may arise from the pain that will be caused if the affair is discovered. But they also may feel guilty because the moral climate or their religious upbringing make it impossible to feel otherwise. No matter how beneficial they may feel the affair to be, as we saw in Simon's case, they will feel guilty.

The impulse to disclose in order to relieve guilt usually backfires. Too often the desire for relief is joined to one for absolution. Of course this presupposes that the spouse will understand and put his or her own feelings aside. People also naively wish their spouses will somehow appreciate the attractions that drew them to the lovers in the first place.

Frequently the impulse to confess is accompanied by the notion that "if I'm brave enough to confess, then my husband/wife will appreciate my courage." And that appreciation might mitigate the sense of betrayal. Of course these expectations are almost invariably misguided. When we turn to the spouse's reaction, we shall see why.

The impulse to confess puts women particularly in a double bind. They feel guiltier, but the consequences if they confess are graver. As Laura said of her policy of secrecy around her affairs: "I might want to have a closer relationship with my husband, but that is not what he is interested in. The kind of relationship we have had for almost twenty years is workable. It does not put pressure on him, the way I used to—to make him talk to me more or to do more 'sensitive' things with me. He is a good husband and father in many ways, but he is just not a confidant. But you don't need it all in the same package, do you? I used to feel lonely a lot. Now I think the way we've worked it out is all right, although it would not work if he found out.

"Sometimes I feel frightened that things might get found out and everything would blow up. And sometimes I feel sad that these affairs actually make me more distant from him and symbolize how I can't be close to him. I think if he found out, I might feel guilty— for the secrecy, especially."

The "if he found out" stops her, for if he did, she thinks her marriage would be over.

Men's confessions engender different consequences. Indeed, some men confess because their affairs become too painful; they actually turn to their wives for comfort. Since wives are usually their main and only confidantes, this is not surprising.

This happened in Phillip and Rachel's marriage. Married for ten years, Phillip began an affair with a younger woman with whom he worked on a political campaign. For most of their marriage Phillip had exalted Rachel, an accomplished and charming woman: "She was always so competent and had all the friends. She had done so much in her life, and she taught me most of what I know about the world and how it ticks. I was never as sure of myself as she was. Even though I knew she also had insecurities, they didn't get in the way of her career and friendships as they did mine." Phillip was marginally successful, tentative and unsure of himself. Rachel organized their social life, kept their finances, and was responsible for housework and major purchases. She had brought her own independent and more substantial income to the marriage.

In his political work Phillip met someone who idolized him and, flattered, he fell completely. For two years he kept the affair secret. In time his lover met someone else and ended their affair. "I was completely shattered. I didn't want to get out of bed. I felt worse than I had before, as if it confirmed that I really wasn't all those marvelous things she had said about me but was this stupid little nothing I'd felt I was before." Despondent, he turned to Rachel. Her response was to mother him. She said she had to put jealousy and betrayal aside until she was sure he would be all right. She claimed, "Well, he was in pain, wasn't he? He wasn't eating or sleeping. We had to get him out of that awful state." They spent many tortured weeks until he began to stabilize. Only then did she permit her own pain to surface. She never thought seriously about divorce.

Women are more likely to leave or be left after disclosure or exposure. The men who stay on find themselves suffering a different consequence—marginalization within the family or becoming the scapegoat. Men, already usually more peripheral to their children than their wives (even if both are working), may be further marginalized as a result of their wives' anger and pain, when they gather their children around them for support. Sometimes they turn their children explicitly against their father.

Barbara, a thirty-three-year-old teacher and mother of three, told of how she and her younger sister grew up distant from their father, whom they had adored; it stemmed from his having an affair when she was ten and her sister eight. Although he left home for a few months, he did return after ending his affair. Her mother never forgave him. One way this was demonstrated was by her mother's pointed exclusion of him from family activities. She organized their social life and outside activities, most of which revolved around things that excluded men, such as sewing, baking, or decorating. If Sunday outings were ever suggested by her father, her mother usually prevented them by diverting the girls to other, more pressing projects. Because of the power and emotional control they have within the family, women are able to marginalize their husbands, while husbands usually do not have that power and cannot do the same.

Others decide to tell because they want their spouse to know what they have learned from the affair. For instance, if someone learns in an affair that he or she can be uninhibited in bed but his or her sex life at home is dull and constrained, there may be a great temptation to say, "Look, this isn't my fault. I found that out in bed with so and so." Linda was greatly tempted to tell Peter about Bill's passion in bed and his excitement in talking to her because Peter dismissed her wish that he be more attentive and passionate as idealistic. She resisted the impulse to tell, but not everybody does.

Even people in segmented marriage models can feel the pressure to confess in this way, because they believe that if they can present evidence to their spouse, he or she might change and the marriage would not have to be segmented anymore. Sam sometimes wishes he could tell his wife about his more passionate sex with other women or that Ellen was more attractive to him because she is spicier, more spirited, and more independent. Then maybe Marlene would change. Again, Sam does not say anything because he knows not only would she not change, but she would also be irrevocably hurt.

Sometimes people confess affairs because they want to end a state of indecision. Daniel wanted to tell his wife about his affair partly because he hoped she would throw him out, and then he would then not have to make the decision to leave and be with Jessica. But he had not predicted the power of his wife's fury. When she became enraged and did throw him out, he backtracked and was horrified at what he provoked. "It hadn't really hit me how she would feel. I think I was assuming that if I was feeling estranged from her, then she was probably feeling estranged from me. I couldn't have predicted that her fury would extend to her threatening to prevent me from being with our kids. I was not prepared for it."

People also reveal their affairs when they want either revenge or to equalize a relationship after their spouse has had an affair. The desire to pay back or to rebalance the marriage emotionally can brew over many years. A few years after Ian, a fifty-year-old physicist, found out that his wife had had an affair, which she claimed was "insignificant," he had an affair—again, "insignificant"—with one of their acquaintances. It was necessary for him to tell his wife. Both understood that it had made something equal again in their marriage and put an end to something that his wife had begun with her earlier affair. Equality of power is a central, explicit issue in their marriage. It is an issue in many matters, such as the time each allots to his or her career and negotiations over who does what with their children. It is not surprising, then, that it was a major dimension in the aftermath of his wife's affair.

The story of Ian and his wife is unusual. The retaliatory or spiteful affair more often results in a tremendous emotional mess. When disclosed, such *quid pro quo* affairs often end with a lot of bad feeling, including the affair partner's feeling exploited or like a pawn in a marital game. And the disclosure does not achieve the desired effect—the sharply targeted suffering of the spouse who had the original affair. Too often other things suffer, including the quality of the marriage and the person who had the retaliatory affair. The process of guilt, betrayal, hurt, and insecurity begins again. Now the retaliator becomes the guilty one (sometimes doubly so, since he or she should have *known* how it feels).

Exposure

Sometimes an affair is discovered even though people have resolutely decided that they will not tell. This occurs through exposure, which is usually the most explosive way for any affair to be revealed. If a spouse chooses to tell about his or her affair, at least he or she is partially prepared for the drama that is likely to ensue. This is not the case in exposure, which is a shock to both spouses and can destabilize a marriage far more. It underscores the deception element of an affair, emphasizing the potential for feeling betrayed. The revelation is unmitigated by an attempt at honesty.

Exposure can occur through a third party's actions (either wittingly or unwittingly). Or it can occur through the spouse who is not having the affair finding evidence. Sometimes it can come through the devices of the affair partner.

Susannah's lover threatened to tell her husband in an attempt to get Susannah to continue their relationship. The knowledge that she had the power to retaliate by blackening his name in his profession made it possible for Susannah to call his bluff and so stop the exposure.

George had numerous affairs in his thirteen-year marriage to Dottie. In the first, Dottie surprised George in bed with a friend of hers. After that she became sensitive to clues. Itemized phone and credit card bills have left trails for her to follow, usually to discover that her suspicions have been correct.

Like disclosure, exposure can be the precursor to a marital dissolution. Disclosure can rock and destroy a marriage. The aftermath can be so painful and ugly that no matter how stable and good the marriage was before, no matter how unimportant the affair, and no matter how beneficial the affair might have seemed, the marriage is destroyed. But some marriages survive, often with help. In Dottie's case, religious conviction kept her married, in the belief that to divorce was a sin.

The Spouse's Reaction: Feelings of Betrayal, Jealousy, Insecurity, and Rage

Because marital ideology proscribes both secrecy and affairs, there is no way to avoid a spouse reacting with feelings of fury, betrayal, jealousy, and insecurity. Both men and women react this way. However, their gender means they will express them differently.

Husbands do not act the hurt, rejected victim as easily as wives. Instead, they smolder with anger, put fists in walls, threaten to kill people. This is even true for calm and gentle men. Henry, a shy and retiring social worker, was married to the extrovert and flamboyant Alicia, who had a history of abusive, tortured relationships, including with her father. Henry came from a stable, bookish, and ordered background. He did a lot of looking after Alicia, calming her frequently ruffled nerves and quick temper. But when Alicia had an affair and confessed it to Henry—to relieve her misery after she had been rejected by her lover—instead of being comforted, she received a smack in the face, which was another abusive experience to bank in her already large account.

Men, like women, do feel hurt, betrayed, insecure, and jealous (which was why Henry hit Alicia), and they act out angrily. Our culture supports men's anger. In contrast, despondence detracts from manliness. Rob and Maria are a case in point. After thirteen years of marriage with no children but a history of emotional distance and unsatisfactory sex, Maria left Rob for another man. When her affair soured, Maria tried to return to Rob. While Maria was gone, Rob had moped around and was depressed, unmotivated, his self-esteem hitting rock bottom. She returned to a man mired in despondence; he never got angry, just depressed. Maria felt pity, and this turned her off.

Women, while also being furious ("hell hath no fury like a woman scorned"), are more generally despondent and hurt rather than angry. This is, of course, consistent with gender role and cultural expectations. We are far less tolerant of a woman angrily divorcing on grounds of adultery—except when the affair is still continuing. Shouldn't she be thinking of her children? The family's stability? Won't she give him another chance? Unlike a man, a woman is supposed to consider family welfare first and not act hastily in anger. Part of the fascination of *Fatal Attraction* was the role reversal: murderous jealousy emanating from a woman, not a man.

On the other hand, a hurt woman gets mountains of sympathy, and her husband is supposed to repent and repay. We have already referred to Richard and Polly's marriage, stuck in the guilty aftermath of Richard's affair. Although Polly and their two teenage children were enraged, her main feeling was of immeasurable hurt. She has been on antidepressants now for years, and Richard has been repenting. He phones a few times a day to see how she is doing; he buys his family expensive vacations, new things, grand gadgets, and in general acts as if it is his duty to repent and coax Polly out of her pain. He has become the family scapegoat; he accepts this as his penance.

Of course wives who discover their husbands' affairs are also angry. But if they show this too much, the support may turn from them to their husbands. When Mary discovered her husband, Eric, was having an affair with one of his ex-students, she went to town with her revenge. She began persecuting the former girlfriend through letters and phone calls. She called her repeatedly at work, leaving explicit messages about the affair. But when she began to expose Eric at his department, the tide of sympathy turned steadily against her. She was deemed "deranged" and "unhinged."

In contrast, when Hugh, also an academic, publicly humiliated his wife and her lover, sympathy ran with him. Without any clear provocation, Hugh punched his wife's former lover at a cocktail party in front of his wife's entire department. Although the party spirit was dampened, after a few weeks Hugh's reputation remained undiminished.

The revelation of a secret affair obviously has the potential for this sort of destructiveness. As we have said earlier, secrecy can both breathe life into and bring death to an affair. We have focused on how its revelation can threaten or even kill a marriage, but it is also important to realize that it can signal its reconstruction as well.

Managing Marital Change after Discovery

Despite these traumas, the exposure of an affair can be constructive in the end for many marriages. If the affair is well and truly over, if both members of the couple want to preserve the marriage and they both want to dissect it, looking for avenues toward change, the prognosis is better. It is also enhanced if there was voluntary disclosure of the affair rather than exposure. Prognosis may be often better if there is marital therapy. A couple needs dispassion as well as a voice to remind them of their agenda with each other: healing the marriage or ending it. Expressing pain and showing remorse may be part of the plan, but it also needs to include decisions about "where do we go from here?" Too often the longer perspective gets lost in the maelstrom of guilt, fury, and insecurity that surrounds the discovery phase. This is why at this point good marital therapy can frequently make the difference between a marriage's death and its rebirth.

After Susie found out about Simon's affair, the couple endured an extremely painful few months. Susie lost weight; both lost sleep, were unproductive, and cried copiously. Both recoiled from divorce. This shared horror enabled them to realize that they would have to try to get over the affair. While not in therapy, they turned to supportive friends, who fortunately did not take sides. Susie's constant questioning as to "why" pressured Simon into finding an explanation both for Susie and for himself. He found the overwhelming appeal of the affair was that it removed him from Susie's inordinate dependence on him.

Susie had trained as a medical researcher under Simon. In the early stages of her career, this had not been a problem, but with middle age coming on them, Simon was clearly moving far ahead of her. Susie remained too identified with him, and as his confidence grew, hers diminished. For Susie this did not feel like a problem, but for Simon it did. In other ways, too, she had woven her life around him. Although a naturally gregarious person, her friendships slowly attenuated, especially after having children. Galvanized by the crisis in her marriage, Susie joined an exercise class, began to see more of her friends, and eventually set up her own office. The quality of her life improved, and, perhaps of greater note to their marriage, Simon was more passionate and demonstrative with her. A few years after discovery of the affair, their marriage had transformed. No longer did they go from arguments, usually initiated by Susie who was feeling neglected, to reunions, to arguments again.

The example of Susie and Simon illustrates four points in the recovery period after an affair has been discovered. The first is that they used the affair to initiate changes in their relationship, rather than allowing it to control their marriage. As a consequence, the affair receded as the marriage changed. Second, they chose commitment to their marriage. Third, they indicated appropriate areas of manageable change and initiated actions to change them. Fourth, they restated their mutual commitment to a clear model of marriage, in this case to the marriage-is-for-everything model.

But in the aftermath of discovery of his affairs, Nick's marriage changed to an open one. He and his wife now have a clearly agreed-upon contract of what kind of affair is permissible and under what conditions. This is because Nick firmly believes that his resentment would crush his marriage if he were forced to be monogamous. His wife rather begrudgingly capitulated.

The statement of a clear marital model is central to recovery. If a spouse wants a monogamous marriage, he or she needs reassurance that there will never be another affair. Thus the marriage must move to a marriage-is-for-everything model. In Nick's case his wife could live with affairs as long as she was assured Nick would not prefer another woman. The reassurance she needed was not about sexual fidelity but about emotional fidelity. Nick is now explicitly bounded to affairs of brief duration, little intensity, and with women who live at a distance.

There is no place for the segmented model, with its secrecy, in the recovery process. The issues of trust, betrayal, and insecurity that surface need to be settled; only then is there space enough in a marriage for a couple to reflect on it and renew their commitment. The spouse who has felt betrayed needs reassurance through increased intimacy, something at odds with the segmented model, which emphasizes autonomy at the discretion of only one of the spouses. The spouse who has felt betrayed needs to continue to protect himself or herself so there is a keen alertness to evidence of any subsequent betrayals. Consequently any subsequent affairs are much more likely to be discovered.

Most marriages will not survive further discoveries, but there are some that do. Keith had eleven affairs that Sandy knew about in their fifteen years of marriage. But Sandy was a staunch Catholic who took her vows seriously, and she preferred to remain married, suffering anew each time she suspected another affair.

Marital Therapy and Managing Marital Change

People may turn to therapy in crises. As we have already said, people who feel upset by affairs may engage a therapist because they find no other safe person in whom to confide. Moving out of the obsession stage, away from the debilitating pain, is very difficult for a couple to manage on its own. That is in part why outsiders often get pulled in. Because therapists are supposedly unbiased and devoted to analyzing sources of problems, they may offer the calm atmosphere and reflection the couple needs.

A couple can weather the post-discovery phase of an affair without therapy, but it is tricky. Christina and her husband did not get professional help and their marriage survived, but two years after discovery there are still rough days. The marital rules are clear: they have moved to a marriage-is-for-everything model. But Christina occasionally feels empty, her husband's pain is still palpable, and she is extremely careful around him. The atmosphere at home is often tense. Yet they feel they have created clear rules for their marriage through the discovery of the affair.

From what has been said up to now it might seem obvious that marital therapy can sometimes be the difference between a marriage's survival and its death after discovery. Because betrayal, insecurity, jealousy, and guilt are powerful and gripping emotions, couples often cannot loosen that grip alone. A therapist is likely to be an outsider, seen in an arena unsullied by past painful associations. Moreover, being in therapy means that the couple is committed in principle to spending regular amounts of time and energy in trying to understand at least the motivation for the affair and its effect on the marriage. Of course, not every therapist provides the dispassion, wisdom, appropriate judgment and tact necessary to the process. And not every member of a couple in therapy wishes to heal his or her marriage.

In addition, most marital therapy operates from the marriage-is-for-everything model and therefore emphasizes intimacy over autonomy. Because of the prevalence of this model, much therapeutic work devotes itself both to moving couples toward monogamy and also to encouraging disclosure of information about the affair, which promotes intimacy, although there is some disagreement about the degree. How much detail is it healthy to hear? To permit secrecy discourages intimacy, the line goes. Openness and honesty are promoted. Intimacy is increased if the couple suffers through the trauma of the affair together, similar to how mourning a painful loss together draws people closer. There is a strong feeling among many therapists that they should not hold marital secrets told them by one member of the couple if they are treating the marriage as a whole. For technical and ethical reasons this is often a sensible stand to take. If the secret comes out and the therapist is discovered to be a party to it, the spouse who feels betrayed also feels betrayed by the therapist. This can undo any past or future work. But, as we have seen, disclosure is sometimes the very thing that wrecks the marriage. In addition, pressuring to disclose can hasten the end of therapy.

When Clark and Lydia were in therapy, the therapist suspected that Lydia was having an affair. He scheduled separate sessions for the spouses in the hope of encouraging Lydia's confession in Clark's absence. Because Lydia suspected this, she cancelled both sessions, and therapy ended.

This is clearly a particular view of the function of marital therapy. As we have said, most marital therapy starts from the view that "marriage should be for everything," and an affair is a symptom of something wrong with the marriage. Consequently, whatever the person got from an affair should probably be gotten in the marriage. The task for the therapist is to get the couple to work on getting it in the marriage. In the case of Richard and Polly, the task was to develop more intimacy, cooperation, shared activities, and interest in each other, since the affair pointed up the enormous isolation between Richard and the rest of his family.

But in Nick's case, therapy that promotes monogamy or the marriage-is-for-everything model would not have worked. His undemonstrative wife felt awkward having cozy, intimate fireside talks every night or throwing her arms around him in public. This was one of the reasons he felt drawn to affairs—they renewed warm connections with women. The couple's compromise was to accept that their marriage was limited and to work out a marital agreement bounding but allowing extramarital affairs. In fact, therapy helped them reach this agreement. The emphasis in marital therapy on the importance of intimacy in a marriage does not acknowledge the competing need for autonomy. Both Nick and his wife had different autonomous needs. His wife wanted to be left alone some nights, unpressured to be demonstrative, just as Nick wanted sexual freedom.

In addition to seeing affairs as pathological or symptomatic of something wrong with a marriage that therapy has to set right, there are therapists, such as Frank Pittman, to whom we referred in chapter 1, who take a strong position against affairs on moral grounds. In his view affairs are a "sickness" in a "sick" marriage.

Other therapists take a different position. They see their task as helping couples to decide whether they want to stay together or not, and if they do, to identify realistic, appropriate, and manageable negotiations they must achieve in order to do this. The model of marriage is up to the couple to decide. Disclosure is not an aim in itself, because it can lead to destruction. If it occurs, it produces a crisis that therapy must manage. Instead, in this view, therapists must weigh the pros and cons of disclosure if they suspect an affair and decide, as the professional helping the marriage, whether to encourage or discourage disclosure.

When Linda and Peter went into marital therapy, at the time Linda was trying to end her affair with Bill, their therapist knew about the affair from an individual session with Linda. She decided against encouraging Linda to confess. Instead, she encouraged Linda to bring what she had learned from her experience with Bill—that she wanted more intimacy, time, and demonstrativeness from her husband—to the therapy sessions. Linda never mentioned Bill. The therapist helped Peter accommodate to Linda's now clarified desires. The therapy was successful using the affair without ever confessing to it.

On the other hand, Tom and Beth came into therapy because Beth suspected that he had had an affair with one of his trainees. The therapist decided not to pressure Tom to confess, although he was pretty sure that Beth was right. In the first session Tom denied it all. In the second he confessed. The moment of the confession was excruciating. Silence fell. Beth seemed to have stopped breathing. Then very quietly she said, "Well, thank you for at least telling me." Another silence ensued. A few moments later, fueled by whatever angry visions she had just conjured up, she began to beat Tom, small fists against a tough, unyielding frame, then collapsed into his arms. He held her and they both sobbed.

For the therapist the question of whether or not to encourage disclosure had been settled. But he then had to cope with the aftermath. He warned them that this was only the beginning. They would come more frequently than before, and he would be on call for them. He explained what each would be feeling, much as we have done in this chapter. And he explained that the work was now going to be focused on why the affair occurred, whether they wanted the marriage to survive, and if so, in what way. What the therapist did was give the couple a long-term perspective, something that Tom and Beth were unable to do.

In order for a therapist to make an adequate assessment of whether to permit or encourage disclosure and to determine what model of marriage to move a couple toward, we think the therapist first needs to try to analyze the affair along specific dimensions. What is the context of the affair—the life cycle, personal history or family script issues, and the history of vulnerability in the particular marriage? What model of marriage has each member of this couple been operating from? And, finally, the gender issues, which we have tried to highlight throughout this book, need to be underscored when treating the marriage.

Men and women use different language and constructs to describe their feelings, motivations, and the impact of the affair. In trying to get the couple to understand their respective reactions to the affair itself and to its aftermath, the therapist must be a "gender broker," the phrase coined by feminist family therapist Virginia Goldner. He or she must interpret each spouse's experience to the other, trying to take each member of the couple over the gender divide, encouraging empathy with the spouse's experience. It is difficult and not always successful work. But therapy sometimes can offer the chance for a wounded marriage to recover.

8

Marriage, Affairs, and Divorce

*All three women are equally upset, equally desperate. All three
men involved have double vision. All seek the conveniences of
marriage and the freedom of the sexual chase. All three women
want sexual joy and security to be combined in the same person:
their image of men is an integrated one. Therefore the desires of
men and women are incompatible. Not because the man's desire
is for the woman and the woman's desire is for the desire of the
man, but because women can't find in men whole human
beings, and the whole human beings women are are not what
men have been led to believe they want.*

Ann Oakley, *Taking It Like a Woman* (1984)

*I*T IS OFTEN TAKEN FOR GRANTED THAT AFFAIRS CAUSE THE
breakup of marriages or, if they are not the cause, that they are at
least a symptom of a dying relationship and so represent a step on
an inevitable path to a divorce. In this chapter we will examine connections between affairs and divorce. We conclude that the conse-

quences of affairs for marriages are not as straightforward and obvious as many believe.

With all that husbands and wives expect from marriage, it follows that an affair will be much more threatening now to the survival of a marriage than it would have been in the past. Since marriage has become more exclusive and the value placed on open communication, intimacy, and a shared sexuality between the couple has grown, other sexual relationships represent a much more potent betrayal and threat. This threat may be further increased if an extramarital relationship shares some of the companionate features of the marriage. An affair may make its own demands for exclusiveness and sharing between the partners. But do affairs always lead to tears?

Affairs and Remarriage

Some affair partners become new spouses through divorce and remarriage. But the journey from one partner to another is only very rarely a simple one. Quite apart from the financial, emotional, and practical difficulties that divorce always brings, as well as the immense upheavals for children, the ending of a marriage always puts great strain on the affair relationship as the new couple tries to convert it into an exclusive marriage.

William described the pain of this process. Both he and his (new) partner were married. Both had children. After a two-year affair they decided to leave their marriages and marry each other.

"I can remember that weekend all too clearly. It was the first time we were together after we had made the decision to be together and end our marriages. Everything was out in the open. Both our partners knew, and we could be together. No secrets. It was a moment we had talked about endlessly. We had decided to go to the country to a place we had visited early in our relationship. The first evening we were both quiet. We were tired, exhausted really, from the weeks of argument and discussion. It was the same the next day. There didn't seem to be any energy between us. We never made love the whole weekend—that was certainly a change. Up to that point we had made love almost every time we were together. We never could wait. That weekend was the end of our relationship."

In fact, as William told the story, they continued together for nearly six months but gradually acknowledged they were both depressed, she particularly. The weight of leaving the two marriages had crushed their relationship. Neither went back to the original partner, or at least not permanently. That weekend was two years ago, but there is still pain in William's voice as he describes it. He now has a new partner (after a number of false starts) and is soon to marry again.

"I feel quite different now—older, wiser I hope. It was a real mess when I first left Joanna. It seemed simple at the time, and I couldn't see why it wasn't working with Joanna." Asked how it might have been if he had met Joanna after his marriage had ended, all he could say was "different."

There is always a degree of interdependence between an affair and a marriage so that the ending of one is bound to have implications for the other. The very secrecy of the affair may be a major element in its attraction. The couple's limited time together and the usually very restricted circumstances in which they meet may help to give the relationship its special excitement and intensity. Everyday life and all its routineness are excluded; the couple is there solely to be together. It is all prime time and, as one of our interviewees remarked, "you don't have to stay to do the dishes."

Affairs are often fed by a sense of what might be. The secrecy and the competing demands of the couple's marriages inevitably mean that there are many things they cannot do together. Not least among these may be idealized features of a marriage, such as quiet evenings together with nothing in particular to do. Once an affair becomes a marriage, romantically imagined futures become present realities, and not all relationships can stand the transformation. The couple may be too dependent on the limitations within which most affairs exist. The imagined possibilities that were always beyond reach may not be quite so wonderful when they become everyday life. For these reasons, when an affair becomes public and the couple begins to extricate themselves from their old marriages to move into a new one, the relationship does not survive. Others may get as far as remarriage or cohabitation before the relationship collapses.

As has been well-demonstrated in surveys from many countries, second marriages are less long-lasting than those of couples on their first time around.

A second marriage that grows out of an affair always has to face an uncomfortable truth at its heart. As both partners commit themselves to a new exclusive relationship, they know that one or both of them has been through that very same process before and that exclusiveness was betrayed. But, of course, they always hope and try to convince themselves that this time it will be completely different and they will surely triumph over experience.

Rachel had been remarried for nearly four years when we talked to her. She had two children from her original marriage and a one-year-old from the new marriage. She and her new partner, Bill, had first met in college and then met again years later when both were married. They then began the affair that effectively ended both their marriages. It was after the remarriage that Rachel began to have questions about Bill's first marriage, and only then did he tell her about other affairs he had had before theirs had begun.

"I thought more and more about that. I thought I had felt secure in the new marriage. It was certainly a great deal better than the first, and I trusted Bill. I tried to talk to him about this several times. It was hard to begin because I did not want him to feel that I was questioning our marriage, but I needed to know *why* he had these affairs. I am not sure I understand even now. He just says how different our relationship is to that with his first wife. I'm pretty sure it is, but I suppose I still want reassurance."

The fear may not always be expressed openly, but it can provide a strong stimulus to rewrite history and to reach an understanding of the earlier marriage that leaves the new partners in the clear. Often, the new story will be that the earlier partner had some quirk of character or behavior that made living with him or her impossible, despite all the best efforts of the spouse, or that the marriage was already dead when the affair began. "She was an impossible person." "I never really trusted him." A solution to these difficulties of transformation that was found by one man was simply to exchange the roles of wife and mistress.

Charles was a successful professional in his early thirties. After seven years of marriage he had become involved with a single woman at his place of work. The affair blossomed in secret for a couple of years, but as time passed Charles came under increasing pressure from his new partner to leave his wife and set up a home with her. "At that point I did not think about leaving my marriage. I guess I was aware that Joan wanted that, but I felt things were okay as they were. She pushed a bit, but I thought she understood my position." He resisted, not least because of his two children and because he felt unable to face telling his own family, who had initially rather disapproved of his marriage. His mother, in particular, had not been happy with his choice of bride, but she had seemed to be won over particularly after the birth of the first grandchild. It was his mother's death that provided the key for Charles to change his situation. Within a few months of it he told his wife about his affair and said he wanted to leave. She was very shocked but gradually came to accept the situation, perhaps more in sadness than anger. Within a few months Charles was established in a new home with his new partner, and as soon as the divorce was finalized, they married.

Charles was very keen to maintain links with his children. As well as taking them for weekends he dropped in to see them during the week. There seemed to be a lot to discuss about the children, so he would arrive before they got back from school to have time to talk things over with his ex-wife. Gradually these talks became rather more intimate, and the couple renewed their sexual relationship. "We just slipped back into it. We knew each other very well. It seemed a natural thing."

When we last had news of Charles, he was two years into his new marriage and had a new daughter. He was also eighteen months into his affair with his ex-wife, which at that time was unknown to his new partner.

People may be convinced that they are right to leave their marriages for their lovers, but they may miscalculate or the affair may fail to weather the transformation phase. The affair and the needs of those involved may have been too dependent on its limitations. Marina, who left her husband after twenty years of marriage for a man who then became her business partner, found that she had traded a life of predictability and security for one of constant turmoil, instability, financial ruin, and emotional abuse. Before she left

her husband she had found her lover exciting, interesting, and chal-
lenging. She had seen herself growing through her relationship with
him, changing from a middle-class, middle-aged, rather dull woman
into a more unpredictable, questioning, and sexually uninhibited
one. For this man she had left her job and marriage and invested a
good deal of her capital in their shared business venture.

Whether she wants to return to her marriage is a moot question;
her husband is not waiting with open arms. But what is clear is that
she does not feel prepared to stand on her own, which she is now
forced to do. She had left her husband for a new relationship with
her lover. She had not left her marriage to be on her own.

Betty's is another story of misjudgment about the durability of
an affair when it transforms into the central and exclusive relationship. Betty was married to Steve for eighteen years. They had two
children, now young teenagers. Steve, a highly controlling and
charismatic man, was the main player in the marriage. Betty had
pushed aside education and career plans, and felt that she was living
in Steve's rather long-cast shadow throughout their marriage. She
became highly dependent on him and received much reflected glory
as his wife.

When Betty met and fell in love with Mark, a teacher, she felt
enormous relief. She did not have to compete with Mark or prove to
him that she was bright and interesting. Within months of their
affair Betty left home, leaving her children with Steve. Enormous
arguments ensued. Betty needed a lot of support and attention.
Mark was exhausted by it and clearly out of his depth. He felt her
children intruded on their relationship, he resented Steve and his
anger, and he was impatient with Betty's depression. Betty, for her
part, felt let down and melancholy, and had trouble accepting her
loss of status, since she was no longer the wife of a respected, highly
successful pillar of their community. Soon Mark was also angry at
Betty for disturbing the peace of his former life.

Betty and Mark's affair had worked because it was limited. But it
did not work as a marriage: Mark was emotionally limited, and Betty
was lost without someone of Steve's dependability, emotional stami-
na, and powerful position.

So, as we see, the transformation of an affair into an exclusive
relationship is a very difficult process. What may make an exciting

relationship within the limits of an affair is very different from the kind of relationship needed to sustain the everyday life of a marriage. When the secrecy and excitement are gone, there is too little left to sustain a joint life.

Do Affairs Cause Divorce?

We do not know exactly how important affairs are as a cause of divorce. Many spouses blame an affair—especially if it involves their partner—as the cause of their marriage ending. But perhaps the affair was simply the stimulus to end an already dead or dying marriage. And, of course, there are all those marriages that continue despite affairs known and unknown to the partners.

The experience of another relationship can convince a spouse that the marriage is so unsatisfactory he or he should leave it. Even secret affairs can lead to divorce. And, of course, when some affairs become known, the other spouse may find the feelings of betrayal and pain unacceptable and decide to leave.

Gender is all-important. Sociologists who have analyzed marriages, such as Jessie Bernard, have found the experience of men and women so different that they talk of his and her marriages, and we therefore need to consider his and her divorces. The circumstances in which men and women leave their marriages are often different, as are the consequences of divorce for each.

When it is the man who takes the active step to leave, it is usually because he has someone else to go to, while for women it is the quality of their marriage and the feeling that it cannot improve that often persuades them to leave. Even when they do have someone else, it is the impossibility of creating a better marriage with the current partner that is their main motive.

Most divorce actions are initiated by women. It would be a little simplistic to suggest that whoever makes the first legal move is always the leaver. It might be, of course, that, having more concerns about the house, money, and children, women are more often in a position where they need to sort out the legal situation, and so they feel impelled to make the first legal move. However, surveys of marriage show that women are generally much more dissatisfied than men. On the other hand, in practical and financial terms, women usually have much more to lose with divorce than men. Just as within marriage they are the homemakers and caretakers of the children, so it is after divorce. The woman will almost always continue to care for and support her children after a marriage ends, but with the difference that economic support will be reduced and she is more likely to be juggling child care with a job. While men may lose their housekeeper and emotional support at a separation, they are usually hit much less hard financially. Indeed, sociologist Lenore Weitzman has argued that men actually gain financially by divorce because maintenance payments are frequently a good deal less than they were paying to support their wives and children in the joint home.

Given that child care is unlikely to be their major preoccupation after divorce, men, unlike their ex-wives, are usually much freer to pursue other relationships. While the picture we have of the lives of single parents is a bleak one with a great deal of unremitting struggle and often poverty, it is perhaps surprising that so many women choose this rather than remain in their unsatisfactory marriages. But that some do leave is a testament to the female commitment to a close, sharing, and intimate relationship—a relationship of a kind that many women fail to find in their marriages.

This is clearly indicated in studies of the complaints that ex-spouses have of their marriages. Those that are uppermost for women concern the emotional and social quality of the marriage. They say that their spouse was distant, not emotionally close enough, that they could not talk to him, that he was not open and would not share his feelings. They did not feel understood or emotionally supported. These features seem much more important than a good sexual relationship for many women. Indeed, some women value sexual intercourse not least because it can bring moments of emotional closeness and sharing. While some complain of their husband's unfaithfulness, this is much lower on most women's list of complaints than the emotional tone of their marriages. Men's lists of dissatisfactions are typically much shorter. It is issues like nagging and bickering, together with their wives' other relationships—including some that are not sexual—that are the important issues for husbands.

These are, of course, complaints from men and women whose marriages have ended. They are marriages where, for whatever reason, spouses have been unable to settle their differences and produce a relationship that meets at least some of their needs. We have described the historical rise of modern marriage and the high ideals it should provide. In the early honeymoon years the ideals of intimacy, companionship, shared time, and an exciting sexual relationship are usually easy to sustain, but as time passes a process of renegotiation gradually comes into play. This negotiation may be seen as a readjustment of the balance between intimacy and autonomy. At first the balance is strongly tipped toward intimacy and sharing, while individual autonomy tends to be pushed aside. But as the first rosy glow begins to fade, other outside interests reassert themselves. There are things each wants to do separately, people to see, relatives to visit, leisure interests, and perhaps above all the world of work, which is usually the male preoccupation.

This process of renegotiation does not always go smoothly, and as one might expect, marriages are particularly vulnerable at this stage, with the highest rates of divorce coming in the early years of marriage. Things will be further complicated if either spouse has an affair during this phase of renegotiation. Because the marriage may seem like a draining and disappointing experience at this time, an affair may feel particularly rewarding. So not only is the contrast between the two relationships likely to be particularly strong, but the energy that goes into the affair is likely to impede or inhibit the marriage's renegotiation process. That can spell the beginning of the end of the marriage. In other cases, however, the affair, provided it does not become too engrossing, can form a stimulus to the renegotiation process. We found cases where this happened, but it is clearly a high-risk strategy.

Recent surveys have pointed to a list of commonsense factors that are related to marriages foundering at this early stage. These factors determine, all else being equal, the likelihood of a couple's successfully renegotiating their marriage relationship. Those who have known each other for a reasonable length of time and have not rushed into marriage are least likely to divorce, as are those whose marriages have the approval, and so presumably the help and support, of the family on both sides.

Age, too, seems important. Those marrying for the first time

when younger than twenty or older than thirty-five are the most vulnerable, but the reasons are probably different at these two ends of
the age spectrum. The young couples are most likely to have less
education and poorer prospects, and they may well lack adequate
material resources and housing for a reasonable start for their marriages. And, of course, their experience of relationships of any kind
will be more limited. While we hesitate to use the term emotional
immaturity for all those who marry young, it may be suggested that
many young couples still have a lot to learn about the conduct of
social relationships. These marriages are often complicated by the
early arrival of children so that, long before the couple has worked
out a satisfactory way of living together, they are coping with pregnancy and child care.

Professional couples are much more likely to delay marriage
until their education is complete—in itself a longer process—and
careers have been launched. Not only does this mean that economically things will be much more secure for them, but it is also likely
that they have had a great deal more experience with varied relationships. But delaying marriage too long brings its hazards—for
reasons that are the opposite of those who marry very young. Those
who have lived on their own for a long time are likely to have developed strong patterns of autonomy and individual needs that they
may find difficult to relinquish, and so it is difficult for them to create the required intimacy to sustain a marriage. It causes too much
upheaval in long-established patterns of living.

The arrival of children brings a whole new set of issues for any
couple because not only do they intrude on the ideal of intimacy
but they also force a division of labor that can run counter to a couple's notion of a shared domestic life. But although satisfaction with
a marriage typically falls after the birth of the first child, couples do
not necessarily become more prone to separate because children
tend to hold couples together. This may be less a conscious decision
that they should stay together for the sake of the children than a
feeling that leaving a family with children is something that should
be contemplated only if things become very desperate and serious.
Increasingly couples are aware of all the problems that divorce can
bring, especially when children are involved.

Adjustments in what were once the ideals for the marriage may bring compromises. Men may make their work the center of their lives and develop more of a social world for themselves around this. Others will put their time and emotional energies into leisure activities. The obsessional quality that men demonstrate in their hobbies, whether it be collecting old jazz records or long hours spent fishing, gives some indication of the emotional energies that may be invested in these activities as a flight from domestic intimacy.

Typically, women make a virtue of necessity and preoccupy themselves with their children. But the cost of the lost ideals of the marriage can be very high, as is indicated by the very high prevalence of depression among married women, especially those at home with children. Research has significantly demonstrated that depression is much more likely to develop where women lack a close and confiding relationship with their husbands. There also seem to be links to the earliest relationship in childhood. Those who become depressed are much more likely to say that they had a difficult relationship with their own mother or that the relationship was disrupted for some reason. As we suggested earlier, those early relationships play a basic role in forming our capacity to build and sustain close emotional relationships in adulthood.

Affairs, Divorce, and the Maturity of Marriage

To understand the possible link between divorce and affairs we need to examine the consequences of affairs in the context of the maturing pattern of marriage. Our difficulty here is not only that we have so little detailed knowledge about who chooses to have affairs but also that affairs are such a varied phenomena, pursued for such varied motives, that it is hard to discern distinct patterns. However, there seems little doubt that those who are having difficulties in renegotiating their marriages after the initial phase may be particularly vulnerable. It is easy to suggest that the pattern is a simple one, that when all is not well at home there is a temptation to seek consolation elsewhere. Doubtless this happens, but the circumstances are usually a little more complex.

For some people, the experience of building a close and confiding relationship has always been within a sexual one. So when intimacy begins to fade within the marriage and is developed elsewhere, the pattern is repeated, and a sexual relationship begins as a way of creating a new intimacy.

Al had a small business of his own that involved printing and display work. He described his eight-year marriage as "average." He enjoyed time at home with his wife and two growing children. He talked little about his work with his wife. He thought she was not very interested, but he did not seem to have tried to find out. The firm did work for a small software company, and Al found himself spending a lot of time with one of its directors, Sheila, who was also married. Sheila was more interested in his work problems.

"At first we just met through business contacts—lunch together or sometimes a meeting to talk about the contract we had, and so on," Al said. "I found I could talk to her about problems in the firm, and that was important to me. In a small company like my own it's often difficult to share your problems with anybody. Eventually we went off to a conference together, and the inevitable happened. Well, I think it probably was inevitable by then. Now [nearly two years after the affair began] we meet from time to time, not that often, because neither of us wants to damage our marriage. I enjoy being with her. I like her company and, yes, I enjoy our sexual relationship. But I don't really think of it as an affair. It's really more of a friendship."

Men are particularly at risk here because they choose women as confidantes. Confidantes may become lovers. Women, on the other hand, turn to other women. Or it may simply be difficult to break old patterns. If the experience and convention before marriage was that most, if not all, intimate relationships became sexual ones, it may be hard to change the pattern when close relationships are formed after marriage. We know that those who have many sexual relationships before marriage are most likely to have them outside marriage too.

There is also the question of opportunity. As the marriage matures and the couple begins to spend less time together, there are more possibilities to meet and spend time with possible affair partners. Opportunity and the phase of the marriage may coincide.

Women who have given up work to be at home with the children may find that when they begin work again, as their children grow up, their marriage may reach a transition point at the same time as they are meeting new people. They may be in a mood for change and for a reexamination of their own relationships.

One of our interviewees, Carol, began a night school course when her youngest began full-time school. The man who eventually became her affair partner was an instructor for another course at the college. Their affair lasted a few months. We spoke to Carol a year later, and she related the following.

"The affair was important to me, not so much as an affair but as part of a kind of reappraisal of where my life was going. I'm now back at work. I have a good job and a good marriage. I don't know if I will ever have another affair. There are great dangers. But that affair was part of a process that jolted me out of a rut, and I don't regret it because of that."

There is some evidence that in recent decades the length of a marriage before a spouse has an affair is getting shorter. Annette Lawson found that those who were married before 1960 who responded to her questionnaire had on average been married for fifteen years before their first affair. This fell to eight years for those married during the 1960s and four years for more recent marriages. But these figures may be somewhat biased because anyone in recent decades who was "postponing" an affair would be outside the sample because the survey covered only people who had already had an affair.

While women may be catching up a bit, there is a general belief that men have more affairs than women. We have already discussed some of the reasons this may be so. A further reason may be that men's affairs are less likely to end their marriages than those of women. We make that statement not simply on the grounds that a continuing double standard makes their affairs more acceptable than those of their wives, but because of some of the typical features of the male affair and how these relate to their marriages. Because of their emotional and sexual development, men are usually much more successful than women in creating compartments in their lives that allow an affair and a marriage to coexist with little apparent connection. Both the way their emotional development involves a necessary separation from the first love relationship, that with the mother, and the way their sexuality is formed outside of a social relationship, mean that for men the separation of an affair from a marriage is more easily accomplished.

It is frequently said that wives can always tell when their husbands are straying, but our interviews suggest that this may well be a myth. And it is not surprising, given men's ability to compartmentalize their lives. We have all heard stories of a chance discovery uncovering an affair that went on for months or years without any suspicion at all. In occasional dramatic cases a husband has established a second home complete with children, a car, and a mortgage without arousing suspicion. In interviews with wives who have suddenly discovered their husband's infidelity, we have been struck by the fact that what often hurts and perplexes them most is that they could not tell that their husband was having an affair.

Alison had a typical story. The chance discovery of a letter led to the uncovering of her husband Steven's two-year affair. She said, "Steven had been working hard for some months, and his work took him away from time to time—or so I thought—but that seemed quite natural at this point in his career. I remember thinking one day after hearing about the breakup of a friend's marriage how lucky we were. We still enjoyed each other and liked to do things together. And he could be so warm and loving. It is very hard now looking back on it to think that through all that time he was seeing someone else. . . . I think in many ways it would be easy to accept now if I *had* suspected, if I had been able to tell something from the way he was with me."

The pattern of men's lives, more often than women's, are split between home and a world of work, which encourages and reinforces the pattern of separate compartments. Here we mean more than that work provides opportunities to meet others and excuses to be away from home. It can be through work that men become practiced in living in two separate social worlds and learn to keep them apart. This means they may feel relatively comfortable about the coexistence of an affair and a marriage. If this statement is correct, we would expect there to be many more men's affairs that remain secret and undiscovered, continuing alongside a marriage and not disturbing it. Most of these are likely to be affairs that will not lead to divorce, unless they are discovered and the wife decides it's time to leave the marriage. But difficulties can arise if there is a discrepancy and there are pressures from the affair partner to make things more permanent.

Malcolm was an academic nearing the end of a long and not undistinguished career. He had been married for over thirty years, and his three children were all out of the house. His wife, Patricia, worked part-time in a library and led a full and apparently satisfying life with many activities and a full social life. They were beginning to talk of retirement and moving to a smaller house in the same city.

Three years earlier Malcolm had met Deborah while traveling to a meeting abroad. She was some ten years younger, a journalist who wrote features for a quality paper. She, too, was married with two children, the youngest of whom was soon to complete her education. Malcolm had had earlier affairs, including one that his wife had discovered, but this one was much more important to him. He felt immediately drawn to Deborah and found it easy to talk to her and to be close. They shared many interests. The affair prospered. Although they lived hundreds of miles apart, the nature of their occupations made it relatively easy for them to meet from time to time. About once a year they managed a week away together.

After about a year they both began to talk of leaving their marriages and moving in together. Malcolm agreed, but as he began to consider the consequences for all the parts of his life, he became more doubtful and kept postponing the final decision. Deborah was ready to tell her husband about the affair and to leave as soon as Malcolm agreed to a date.

At this point Malcolm's wife discovered the affair through a friend's chance meeting with Malcolm and Deborah. When confronted by his wife, Malcolm admitted the relationship but said that, although it had been going on for some time, it was not serious. Patricia was not so sure; she saw Deborah as a threat to her marriage. She wanted the marriage to survive and set about making sure that Malcolm would stay. She played on his guilt. In as many ways as she could she tried to show him how much he would be giving up if he left and how uncertain his future life would be with Deborah. But Deborah fought back, and for several months the two

women, in their different ways, pushed their cases. More than anything, Malcolm wished to preserve the way his life had been before
the discovery. Slowly and painfully he came to realize that he could
not give up his marriage and the life that surrounded it, and to preserve it, he would have to end the affair. "In the end I suppose you
could say I voted for my marriage. I wanted both, but the marriage
came first." It took him a long time to get to that point. Patricia
knew that time and history were on her side.

Because wives are indeed part of the status quo and will usually
be the emotional and social housekeepers as well as the providers of
bed and board, men find it hard to leave marriages even when their
relationship with their wives has become very unsatisfactory. But
through compartmentalization and splitting they can find intimacy
and more satisfying sex and love elsewhere. Women, on the other
hand, find this more difficult because for them splitting is much
harder. Despite the much greater practical difficulties of leaving a
marriage, for them an affair may be a more serious threat to a marriage. But as we have already noted, this does not necessarily mean
they will leave a marriage for an affair partner. Perhaps more commonly, the affair begins a process of evaluation which eventually
leads to them leaving their marriage. As we have pointed out, they
are likely to be dissatisfied with more things in their marriage.

Jane, a doctor's wife, had been married for nearly fifteen years.
The youngest of her three children was now safely established in elementary school, and Jane was back working part-time in a design studio. At that point she said she felt okay about her marriage. Her
husband, Dick, was a little distant from her at times, and she did not
particularly like to spend time with his work colleagues. But he was
good with the children, and they seemed to function well as a family. Through her work Jane met another designer who was in town for
a few weeks. Dick happened to be away for part of this period, and
she and her designer colleague spent a lot of time together.

"I liked him," Jane said. "He was easy to talk to and was interested in my work—something I don't think was true of Dick. After
spending an evening with him, we slept together. It wasn't great
passion. I think I was interested to see what it would be like more
than anything. But it was lovely to be with someone who seemed to
care for me and wanted me."

They kept in touch—"more friends than lovers, I think"—but distance made it hard for them to meet.

Some months later Jane began a second affair with a colleague at the studio where she worked. This time it was real passion, and it was not long before James, her new lover, was asking her to leave her marriage and live with him. "I was certainly tempted, but it seemed an impossible step to take." She continued to hesitate but decided to tell her husband what was happening:

"The whole thing exploded, and within a couple of weeks the affair was definitely over. James's wife was told, and on one awful evening we all met together. James quickly decided that he wanted to stay put. The way he behaved then certainly reinforced my doubts about him. Dick and I spent hundreds of hours talking. He was angry, of course, and I don't think he ever understood how I felt. He saw it all as a need to rearrange our domestic routines while I wanted the basis of how we were together to change."

Jane described how these discussions, at least in retrospect, were the beginning of the end of her marriage. It was nearly two years before they separated. Now she lives on her own with her children. "I am a new woman now. It's been hard and painful, especially for the children, but most of the time I am sure I did the right thing."

We may have come a long way since the attitudes of the last century regarding infidelity, but double standards do persist. In general, women remain more tolerant of their husbands than husbands do of their wives. Some wives may be fairly certain that their husbands are having an affair but, provided it is discreet and does not impinge on their marriage, they do not ask and the husbands do not tell. For a few there is a more or less tacit agreement—not an open marriage in the sense we discussed earlier, but an acknowledgment that if he is away and he sleeps with someone, that is acceptable. Perhaps surprisingly, the advent of AIDS does not seem to have had much influence on these attitudes. Indeed, as we have noted, the advent of the HIV virus, as yet at least, seems to have had little influence on affairs.

Male tolerance of their wives' affairs is much more limited. Where there are agreements, tacit or explicit, the motives are not always reciprocal. Men who enter such agreements seem to do so as a necessary price they have to pay for their own sexual freedom.

They still feel sexual jealousy very acutely. Some marriages are stuck in a kind of frozen distance where the husband harbors a continuing unspoken resentment and hostility because his wife has slept with someone else. Retaliatory affairs may be part of this male pattern, but these are usually kept secret to avoid confrontation and anger and because knowledge of them would detract from the power the husband feels he gains from the deception. While we have examples of this pattern—where it is a wife who feels resentful about her husband's affair—the patterns seem much more common the other way around. Curiously, however, such marriages seem very stable, at least in the sense that they persist.

The continuing double standard and the power of male sexual jealousy mean that there are usually greater dangers to a marriage when wives' affairs become known than those of husbands. Their affairs may become known more often because they are less practiced in splitting off the two relationships. Also, because their lives are more home-based and they do not have the convenience of excuses related to work, they may run more risks of discovery. Wives' affairs are more prominent among the issues that men bring up at divorce. Once again we must emphasize that it is not possible to say exactly what role they play as causes of divorce. While affairs may certainly be seen as breaking points, it is our impression that the affairs of women, like those of men, are not in themselves a major cause of divorce.

The popular myth is, of course, that love conquers all, that married people (but less often married men) may, if they meet the right person, fall in love. And in spite of their spouses, children, and home, men are forced by uncontrollable passion to give up everything to be with their lover. This view regards love as a kind of external affliction that, unannounced and unexpectedly, can cause people to take leave of their senses and behave in abnormal ways. It is certainly not difficult to find people who have left a marriage to be with someone else and who speak in these kinds of terms.

As social scientists we would not wish to deny the experience of feelings that our profession has so singularly failed to analyze or understand very well. However, love has come to be seen as the justification for relationships in our culture. It has come to represent something even more powerful than marriage. Not only is love now a required condition for marriage, but it can also be a justified reason for leaving it. We come back once again to the contradiction of our ideal of the companionate marriage. Love is regarded as a sudden, unpredictable state that overtakes people and leads them into marriage. Unless the state of matrimony inoculates against any subsequent attack, it may strike again. Following its imperative will lead people from one marriage to another. But our rather more prosaic view is that most of those who leave their marriages for others do so because they have failed to find what they wanted and hope they will do better with someone else.

9

Conclusions

*A marriage, so free so spontaneous, that it would allow of wide
excursions of the pair from each other, in common or even in
separate objects of work and interest, and yet would hold them
all the time in the bond of absolute sympathy, would by its very
freedom be all the more poignantly attractive, and by its very
scope and breadth all the richer and more vital—would be in a
sense indestructible, like the relation of two suns which, revolv-
ing in fluent and rebounding curves, only to recede from each
other in order to return again with renewed swiftness into close
proximity—and which together blend their rays in the glory of
one double star.*

    *It has been the inability to see and understand this very sim-
ple truth that has largely contributed to the failure of the
monogamic union.*

Edward Carpenter, *Love's Coming-of-Age* (1896)

SINCE THE NINETEENTH CENTURY MANY REFORMERS HAVE
argued, like Edward Carpenter, that monogamous marriage is a
prison that stunts love and the human spirit, especially for women.
The early critics were responding to the rise of companionate marriage, which they viewed as damaging because it reduced the autonomy of the spouses for the sake of the ideals of their shared life. For
some of these reformers, although they did not always argue the
point directly, sexual exclusiveness was part of what they objected

to. They saw the churches and the state as enemies forcing monogamous marriage on the population through marriage and divorce laws, denial of sex education to young people, censorship of information about sexuality, banning of contraceptives, and an educational system and economy that made women economically dependent on men. It was this compulsion toward monogamous marriage that these critics disagreed with, rather than monogamy itself. Indeed, their claim was that if unions could be freely entered into, love would blossom and long-term relationships would remain mutually satisfying perhaps over an entire lifetime.

Some also emphasized the need for easier divorce so that when marriages did go wrong or were entered into without sufficient consideration, the couple could be free to try again. Beyond that, they felt that if divorce was possible, it would improve the quality of marriage, as this essayist wrote in 1900:

> *If people could divorce themselves at will and without publicity, they would be as careful to preserve each other's esteem after as they were before marriage. We should then seldom see what so frequently happens now; the charming, neat, obliging fiancée, developing into the giddy, careless, slatternly, and disobliging wife, or the ardent and devoted lover cooling down into the neglectful and heartless husband. Those truly married would continue to do all they could to please each other, and those superficially united would practice the outward decencies of married life from mutual and self interests. Marriage would cease to be the grave of love, and the sum total of human happiness would be immensely increased. Possession during good behavior is far better for our weak human nature than possession absolute.*

What would these nineteenth-century critics make of present-day marriage? The elements that they saw as essential for satisfactory marriage have now been more or less achieved. We have divorce on demand; contraception and abortion are generally available, as is information of all kinds about sexuality. Economic pressures on women to marry no longer exist, at least in the sense they did at the beginning of the century. There is freedom to pursue sexual relationships before marriage and to cohabit without it. But have we achieved the ideal marriages the early reformers hoped for? Has the loving fulfillment they argued for replaced the prison they so eloquently criticized?

Throughout the present century, while the external pressure for marriage and the constraints on it have declined, paradoxically the institution has grown in power. Today it is less the churches and state that strive to maintain standards for marriage but couples themselves who set their own ideals for an exclusive, loving, companionate marriage. As sexual relationships before marriage have become general and largely accepted, not just between those intending to marry but for all, there has been a growing need for couples to mark off marriage as a very special kind of relationship. This has been done by putting an increased emphasis on the wedding itself, as well as elevating the ideal of the exclusive monogamous marriage. In a sense, then, the historical shifts in marriage are a consequence of changes in relationships outside, and especially before, marriage.

The freedoms provided by the new attitudes and the availability of contraception have made sex part of many more kinds of adult relationships. These have pushed marriage away from the open model envisaged by the early reformers and toward the closed exclusive ideal that we find today. That situation gives present-day marriage the contradiction that lies at the heart of this book. It is the contradiction displayed issue by issue in magazines such as *Cosmopolitan*, but without acknowledgment or any attempt at its resolution. Side by side these magazines print articles on such topics as "When Is Sex Right?" and "Should You Sleep with Him on the First Date?" for the unmarried, with others that chart the consequences and difficulties of affairs for the married. The clear message is that while sex is fine for the unmarried with a variety of partners, to stray from the marriage bed is fraught with danger. And to confuse matters further, these magazines, unlike the turn-of-century marriage-manual authors, advocate openness and honesty in all matters in marriage, while we know that most affairs remain secret.

There is little sign that we are moving toward any resolution of this basic contradiction. Throughout the period in which companionate marriage has grown and become the norm, there have always been advocates of open marriage, but despite well-publicized examples, the model has never extended beyond a very small minority. Many people do not want to give up their hopes for marriage. They want to hold on to the romantic ideal and the security they hope monogamy will bring.

Open marriage seldom receives institutional support from the marriage gurus—the counselors and therapists. Indeed, these groups may attempt to uphold the contradictions of the exclusive companionate marriage. The marriage menders promote monogamy and regard affairs as a problem, if not a sign of pathology, that must be removed to bring the couple back to the straight, narrow, and healthy life. Secrets are not to their liking, and many refuse to work with a couple if one member has disclosed an affair to them that has not been revealed to the spouse. Indeed, the relationship between therapist or counselor and client shares many of the characteristics and contradictions seen in the marriage relationship itself.

While it would be unfair to say all these professionals are promoters of current contradictions, there is little sign that they are close to devising constructive solutions to present-day dilemmas. But with or without their help, open marriage seems all too fragile. Perhaps we are stuck with the model of exclusiveness as long as this same characteristic remains the basis of our first love relationship—that with our mothers.

Earlier in the book we pointed to the connections between the pattern of mother-child attachment and that of marriage. There are a few signs that the exclusiveness and "monogamy" of mothers' relationships with their infants in our society has been diluted a little; children are beginning to experience a richer variety of relationships, but changes are still minimal. While we do not wish to suggest that these early patterns determine all that follow and in that sense adult relationships are unchangeable, we do want to draw attention to the close historical and cross-cultural parallels between the exclusiveness of mother-baby attachments and the ideal for adult heterosexual relationships.

One recent shift in behavior that can be interpreted as a response to the contradictions of modern marriage is the avoidance of marriage altogether. The twentieth century has been a time when more of the population has married and at an earlier age. But since the 1970s these trends have reversed. The age at which people marry is rising, and the marriage rate is falling.

These changes are explained partly by the rise in cohabitation and partly by the fact that more people are living on their own. Living together became a significant phenomenon in the late 1960s. Then, as now, it was largely found before and after marriage. Most of those who cohabited eventually married, although not necessarily with the person they first cohabited with. Or those who cohabited were divorcées, but this group, too, often married in the end. A common pattern was for cohabiting couples to marry when they had children. But this link has weakened, and an increasing number of children are born to unmarried cohabiting couples. So we can say that at least to some extent living together is beginning to replace marriage. This seems particularly true for the previously married. Perhaps for this group experience has begun to triumph over hope.

These trends toward cohabitation have gone much further in Scandinavia, where marriage is rapidly becoming a minority preoccupation, and almost as many children are born outside marriage as within it. Adults living singly represent another response to the contradictions of marriage, if we assume, as seems reasonable, that most of them have sexual relationships.

How far does cohabitation represent an attempt to rewrite the rules of marriage and so avoid some of the contradictions? Here we are stuck for lack of information. Despite its prevalence, we have no good large-scale studies of people who are living together. Such indications as there are do not suggest that, in general, the rules for cohabitation are very different from marriage. Ideals for exclusiveness are high, and although doubtless there are couples that have negotiated rules for other relationships, the general pattern seems to be of an ideal of monogamy indistinguishable from marriage. This, of course, raises the question of why these couples do not marry or, alternatively, why others do.

There seem to be two main pressures that lead couples toward marriage. The first comes from their families. Attitudes toward marriage are more traditional among the older generation, and the young may feel strong pressures to get married. And to "do it for the parents" may allow the couple to maintain their stance of organizing their own lives in their own way without being seen to bow to societal pressures. It is more a case of pleasing their close kin than conforming to an expectation of society. The second pressure comes from the couple themselves. Evidence continues to suggest that marriage is viewed as a demonstration of a greater commitment. So for many, living together remains a prelude to marriage, albeit one that may last for several years. While marriage clearly maintains its symbolic importance, in legal terms its power has disappeared. We now have what is effectively divorce on demand.

At what point does a couple who live together decide to marry? Obviously situations are very varied, but often marriage follows a change in the couple's life—a pregnancy, a career change, or a move. For others it may come as an attempt to resolve a problem in their relationship. A number of the couples we talked to got married in the aftermath of an affair. They saw the commitment of marriage as a way of avoiding such problems in the future.

Alex and Cheryl had been living together for nearly three years when they married. Both have professional jobs with reasonable salaries. As Cheryl said, "Originally we moved in together because I needed somewhere to live. We had been going together for some months, and I had to move out of where I was living because the lease ended.

"We never really sorted out the basis of our relationship. We did see other people, but I took it for granted that serious sex was out. Alex didn't, or so I discovered later. It all came to a crunch over a relationship he was having with someone at his job. I realized something was going on, and I challenged him. He told me. I was very hurt, but I wanted our relationship to continue. We talked and talked and eventually agreed to stay together. He had to end the relationship. After that we decided to get married. Perhaps we should have done that much earlier. It does make a difference." It seems more likely, though, that such a tactic will lead to a postponement of problems rather than their avoidance.

A striking feature of the accounts of affairs given by many married people is that they claim they still believe in monogamy. This is particularly true for women. It doesn't seem as if they are saying they would like to be monogamous but are unable to live up to it, but rather they are claiming that their affair does not break their commitment to remain faithful or at least stay in the marriage. These affairs are not intended to threaten the marriage, and therefore they are almost always kept secret. Sometimes they are explained in terms that suggest they do not really count: "It was just sex." "It's not real life; it's like going to the movies." This seems another way of squaring the circle of modern marriage, and it can be seen as a particular strategy of the segmented marriage that we described earlier.

Another strategy some adopt is to turn the affair into a marriage, so serial monogamy, albeit with a little overlap at the beginning and end of each relationship, becomes a way of resolving the contradictions. But this strategy carries huge emotional and financial costs, especially if there are children involved. While new ways of sorting out the practical consequences of divorce, such as mediation, may reduce some of the trauma, they can never abolish the upheavals and problems that any change in a live-in relationship brings. But despite these all-too-obvious difficulties, there is a small number of people who marry and divorce repeatedly.

We have already said that people may have strong needs for an exclusive, all-embracing marriage relationship as a result of their early experiences with their mothers. Are there ways in which these needs can be modified so that patterns of marriage are less demanding? If we expected less of marriage, perhaps some of its contradictions could be reduced. While many young people give a lot of thought to marriage and to the way they want to live their lives, the belief in an exclusive marriage-should-be-more-or-less-for-every-thing model remains very strong.

One group that we might expect to have rather different views are young people who have had the experience of seeing their parents divorce. More than most, one might expect this group to use their experience to avoid some of the pitfalls for themselves. Up to a point, surveys of the attitudes of the children of divorce suggest this is true. These young people often begin with a whole range of reservations about marriage. They say you have to be very sure before you commit yourself or that you should wait until you are older and have had the experience of several relationships. But what people say and what they do are not always the same, and this seems to be the case for children of divorced parents. Looking at the eventual patterns of marriage of these young people, we see what appears to be a contradiction. While they often express more caution about marriage than those whose parents did not divorce, they marry at an earlier age and, perhaps because of this, are more likely to divorce in the early years of their marriages.

The explanation for this apparently contradictory behavior is that this group tends to begin their sexual life and live in relationships at an earlier age than those whose parents remain married. This seems to be because they leave home at a younger age and end their education earlier—both factors associated with an earlier start to sexual relationships. Once into relationships and then into cohabitation, they are "at risk" of marriage. The pressures are on them to convert their cohabitation into a marriage, so they end up married earlier than those who begin their relationships later. All their good intentions about caution seem to be set aside once they get into a serious relationship. Perhaps that is the very situation that lies at the heart of our central contradiction in marriage. In the heat of passion and love, it is easy to promise everything and mean it. The model of the exclusive "until death do us part" is ever present, and how can you offer a lover less? But patterns can change.

As we have described, the marriage of today that causes us so much pain and difficulty is little more than a century old, and it does not rule everywhere. In southern Europe and in the Middle East we can find different patterns of marriage that are a lot more stable than ours. In many of these societies, marriage is much more of an agreement between two families and, for the couple themselves, may not constitute their closest confiding relationship. These are societies in which the gender divide cuts even deeper than in our own, and close confiding relationships usually remain within one's own gender—a wife with her mother, sister, mother-in-law, or aunt and a husband with his male friends and relatives. It would be silly to suggest that we can transport a marriage pattern out of the society in which it is a part into our own, but by looking elsewhere at how marriages work, we can build a base from which to reflect on our own society. And reflection is needed if we are to solve our current problems.

Western companionate marriage is very far from the universal ideal; it is a recent invention that appears to offer security and support in a fleeting and uncertain world. For many, its initial promise is short-lived. Some are able to renegotiate and create a more sustainable alternative, while others falter and seek the same illusions elsewhere. Affairs are as old as marriage. But when marriages become companionate and are based on romantic love, their power to erode becomes greater. It is that bittersweet model of modern marriage that lies at the heart of our difficulties.

Perhaps we should leave the last word to one of our younger interviewees. Derek is twenty-seven. He has been married for five years, has a two-year-old son, and recently learned that his wife is pregnant. In the interview he described how he had had "many" relationships before his marriage but at the time of his wedding believed that it was important not to "mess around."

"You believed you should be faithful?"

"Oh, yes, both of us did."

"Were you?"

"Yes. For the first three years of the marriage. I didn't find it particularly difficult. I wanted to be with Nell. We had a great time together. No complaints. Then James was born. That was really important to us both. I became a very 'home' person. Enjoyed being a father—and the marriage. When James was a few months old I was away on a work thing. I met this girl. It was a one-night stand. I never saw her again. I felt pretty terrible about it afterward. At one point I decided I should tell Nell. But I didn't. I can't deny that I enjoyed that night. Perhaps it's just variety. Or maybe I needed a break from my domestic life. Either way I decided I shouldn't ever do it again. But I have."

"Tell me about that.

"I have had three more relationships since then. I suppose you would call them casual. At least two of them. The other is still going on."

"Is that one serious?"

"I don't think so. We meet through our work. Perhaps every month or two. It's something we both enjoy."

"No strings?"

"No."

"And your marriage?"

"I don't see a real problem. Nell doesn't know. She won't. I don't feel great about that, needing to deceive her. But we are happy."

"What about the future?"

"My marriage *is* important to me. So who knows about the rest?"